CW00781497

CULLYKHAN

TROUP CASTLE

AND

FORT FIDDES

ALEX McKAY

With Best wishes
Happy digging

Alex McKay

September 2017

1880

BANFFSHIRE FIELD CLUB

First Edition 2017
Published by
BANFFSHIRE FIELD CLUB
A Registered Scottish Charity (SC015944)

E-mail: bfc.1880@gmail.com
Website: banffshirefieldclub.org.uk
Design & Layout: Roy Milligan

All rights reserved. No part of this book may be used, stored or transmitted in
any form without the express written permission of the publisher.
A catalogue record of this book can be obtained from the British Library.

ISBN 978-0-9524239-4-2

©2017 Alexander McKay

Printed by MMS Almac Ltd, Keith, Banffshire AB55 5DD

Front Cover: Cullykhan, headland to the left, and bay from the car park.

CONTENTS

LIST OF ILLUSTRATIONS

ACKNOWLEDGEMENTS

Unless credited below, Alex or Jennifer McKay took the photographs.

Moira Greig has generously approved the use of a number of photos and illustrations on pages 4, 7, 20, 22, 23, 31, 91, 100 and 112.

Thanks are also due to the following for permission to reproduce under licence:-

Aberdeenshire Council Archaeology Service: page 5
OS under licence No. 100020767 (Crown Copyright) and page 102.

Historic Environment Scotland: page 21 (copyright Helen C Nisbet) and page 72.

National Library of Scotland: maps on pages 25, 26 and 45.

Aberdeenshire Museums Service: page 52.

National Trust for Scotland Photo Library: pages 82 and 83.

The Archives of the University of Aberdeen:
pages 87, 94, 108, and 128 (ref. ABDUA:30094) courtesy of the University of Aberdeen Museums.

The Royal Engineers Museum, Library & Archive:
page 111 & rear cover (ref. 9309.15).

In addition:-

The Friends of Kinloss Abbey approved the use of the image on page 49.

Wikipedia Commons is the source for pages 48, 53, 62 (Bill Reid of English Wikipedia), 75, 76, 106, and 107.

PREFACE

In July 1964 I entered a new world. A few weeks before, some teachers at Banff Academy had taken a group of pupils, including me, on an evening excursion east from Banff, through Macduff and further along the coast beyond Gardenstown. We stopped at two places. The first was a headland, called Cullykhan, where Colvin Greig and Bob Cairns, lecturers from Aberdeen College of Education, told us about the archaeological dig they planned there. They were the co-directors and were seeking volunteers. The second stop, a couple of miles further on, was in the village of Pennan - whose telephone box had not yet become famous in the film 'Local Hero' - where we would be based, staying in the former school and schoolhouse at Auchmedden at the top of the steep brae down to the village.

The view from the car park; the headland where excavation took place is to the left of the bay and beach, with Pennan Head in the distance.

Fortunately, neither a lack of knowledge of archaeology nor what a dig involved were considered impediments. Most of us volunteered. Those who go on excavations either love it or don't come back. I was undoubtedly in the former group. The planned stay of one week extended to the whole four week season; and then the next year ... until digging stopped in 1972.

Looking back I know how fortunate I was to enjoy these positive experiences, not to mention the fun, at an important and formative time in my life. The skills and knowledge gained, a lot of which were unconnected to archaeology, were principally due to Colvin Greig who became sole director in 1966. He and his wife Moira became good friends.

A few years ago, Colvin asked if I would be interested in helping with the historical research on the castle excavated at Cullykhan to help prepare the final report for publication. A number of interim reports had been published, but there was a need to complete the process.

In the years between the end of the dig and this request, I had visited the area many times. These visits usually included a walk over the site. It seemed a good idea to return to a place that had always felt special for me. Perhaps if I had realised how long it would take a beginner to conduct the research, I might have hesitated before agreeing.

The caption for this photograph in the Banffshire Journal of Tuesday August 10, 1971 reads 'Alex McKay, site supervisor at the Cullykhan dig, showing visitors the crucible which was found last week.'

Sadly Colvin died before I had made much progress but Moira has ensured that the excavation reports have been completed and published, a significant achievement as well as a fitting memorial.

Many aspects of the research have been fascinating. For example, looking at photographs of the excavations brought back memories, and pointed up how much had been forgotten. My mother had saved a few cuttings, and subsequently I have found more in back numbers of the *Press & Journal* and the *Banffshire Journal*. One of the striking aspects of these is the number of people – predominantly local folk – who visited the dig on its open days. One report in August 1971 in the *"Banffie"* talks of 2,000 visitors for the recent Public Day.

The corresponding report in the same newspaper in August 1967 does not give an estimate of numbers at the Open Day. It does point out, however, that parts of the excavation were under a foot of water which diggers were bailing out; sadly this was not a unique event during the years of the dig.

For me, the need to contextualise people, events and places has meant that I have read extensively on historical and related topics, certainly more than I anticipated at the outset. The continuing urge to see Troup in a wider context led me to explore themes such as castles in north-east Scotland, coastal castles, Comyn castles; to name but a few. A full exploration of such topics would have extended this study too far, but I am sure that further insights would be gained from such work given, for example, the ever-growing extent of knowledge gained from new techniques used in archaeology and the expanding volume of historical research.

However, I did learn more than was needed for the published archaeological report on the Castle Site. This book attempts to put the knowledge gained from my researches together in a way which will be of value to those who have an interest in the historic Banffshire coast.

Many people have helped me along the way and it is important to acknowledge my debt and appreciation to them.

Any research such as this necessitates visits to libraries and archives, even though a growing amount of material can be accessed online. Staff at the National Library of Scotland, Aberdeen City Library, the Society of Antiquaries Library in the National Museum of Scotland, and the A K Bell Library in Perth have been consistently helpful. Similarly staff at national and local archives, especially in Aberdeen and Aberdeen University, provided valuable service and, often, helpful insights. The Map Library of NLS in Edinburgh is a continuing joy to visit or access online; it is a truly wonderful resource.

The library I have used most frequently is at the Strathmartine Centre in St Andrews. The generous support and advice received there from

Barbara Crawford and Bob Smart has been of great value; their encouragement has been most welcome.

Working with Moira Greig on the publication of the final report on the Castle Site maintained the momentum to continue these researches. Other friends have helped - sometimes inadvertently - by listening to my rambles or reading drafts and making helpful or encouraging noises. Some must be named here. George Clark, a long-standing and valued friend, has experiences of Cullykhan also stretching back to 1964. Ed Knipe, who has spent a lot of time in Gamrie over the years, was of particular help with sources on the Gardens of Troup. John O'Neill's local knowledge and help in setting up the boat trip from Gardenstown to to see what the area looked like from the sea must also be noted. More recently, the support from members of the Banffshire Field Club, especially Roy Milligan, has been much appreciated. It is a particularly happy coincidence that the resumption of publishing by the Field Club has enabled this publication to reach fruition in Banffshire.

Colvin Greig

During the long gestation of this research, my wife Jennifer has been a great support – listening to my latest findings and theories, watching parts of our home disappear under papers, books, maps and plans, and always offering helpful suggestions. Latterly, her own work on the place names in the Troup area has shed important new light, and has also given us further excuses to revisit the area. It is a great pleasure to include that work here.

However my greatest thanks are to the late Colvin Greig, a gifted musician and teacher, a fine archaeologist, and a wonderful person.

Many people I have met have added to my knowledge; that has been an important part of the research. If you wish to comment, please contact me via the email address below.

Alex McKay
April 2017

e-mail: amcksing65@gmail.com

1. INTRODUCTION

Anyone who took part in the excavations used the name Cullykhan for the coastal headland at the heart of this story. Most of us still do, as do many local people. But it is not a name attached to the headland on any map. The name Cullykhan is given to the sheltered bay to the east of the headland. If the headland is named, it is called Castle Point. The significance, and derivation, of the name Cullykhan will feature in the chapter on place names.

The headland lies to the east of Troup Head roughly halfway between Banff and Fraserburgh at the eastern end of the parish of Gamrie in historic Banffshire, modern Aberdeenshire (NJ 8378 6617).

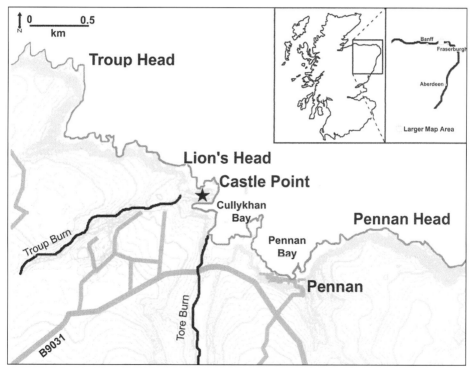

Location of Cullykhan

From 1964 to 1972, under the direction of the late Colvin Greig, a range of excavations took place there. Over that period a significant proportion of the promontory was explored.

The three publications by Colvin Greig about the excavations (see Bibliography) provide more detail about the nature of the extensive human activity on the site, and were the starting point for the research which has led to this publication. A fourth, more recent, report on the Castle Site on Cullykhan by Moira Greig, to which this research has contributed, was published in 2013 (Greig M, 2013, 301-28). A final report by her is in preparation on the prehistoric archaeology on the site.

There has been human activity on Cullykhan from neolithic to modern times. The evidence suggests that during some phases of occupation these were significant settlements, although undoubtedly there were periods when the site was not occupied continuously. A summary of the main archaeological findings on the site is included in the next chapter.

View of headland from car park.

The research described here began with the principal intention of finding out about the people who lived in the various phases of the medieval castle excavated on the site. As described below, that encompasses the period from the late sixteenth century to the early seventeenth century. In that historical period, it was known that two family names were linked to the lands of Troup, the Keiths and, before them, the de Trops. Trying to find more detail about these families, and individuals within the families, was the first priority for the research.

Questions about the castle were easy to formulate.

> When was it built and by whom?
> Who lived there at various times?
> Where did they come from?
> Was occupation continuous?
> Who modified it?
> When and why was the castle abandoned?

Answers to these questions are the central theme of this book.

However, early in the research, it became clear that finding the answers would not be straightforward. The historical sources with details about the castle and people of Troup were not plentiful. Partly as a result of this scarcity, the scope of the research extended in a variety of ways. Broadly these fell into two categories – consideration of other features on the site at Cullykhan, and the broader contexts of Troup and its position in relation to events in north-east Scotland and Scotland in the period under consideration.

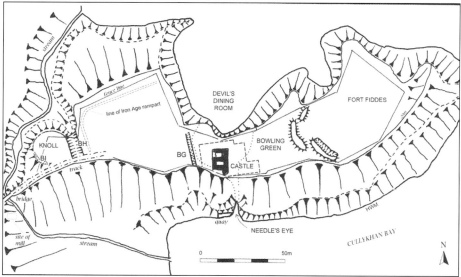

This plan was published in the Proceedings of the Society of Antiquaries of Scotland (PSAS) Vol. 142 and shows the locations of the key areas of historic and archaeological activity on the site. The choice of position for the castle, at the narrowest point and above the fault running through the headland, is clear. Ditches are marked at BG, BH and BI. The truncation of the Knoll caused by modern access in a narrow area is noticeable. The remains of some of the ramparts of Fort Fiddes are marked clearly.

The first of these relevant features on Cullykhan is the existence of a twelfth century house on the Knoll, the term used by the excavators to refer to the first part of the site encountered when going on to the headland. An archaeological report was published in 1989 on this (Greig & Greig, 1989, 279-96) but a reference found early in the researches offered the possibility of identifying people who might be associated with this house. Clearly this was worth pursuing.

These historical researches add to the archaeological evidence already published by suggesting who may have been involved on the Knoll. The outcomes and discussion also served as a potential introduction to the main research on the occupancy of the castle.

Another feature on the headland is the remains of Fort Fiddes, the ramparts of which have been followed in part by the modern fence at the opposite end of the promontory from the Knoll. My initial intention was to exclude Fort Fiddes from the research. Although there was some uncertainty about its date, it was clear that it was post-medieval and after the abandonment of the castle. Indeed, the year 1654 for a long time served as the endpoint of the research. It is well documented, for example in the *Records of the County of Banff 1660-1760* by J Grant (1922), that Alexander Garden acquired the Troup estate in 1654, becoming the first Garden of Troup. He quickly established the first Troup House, not on Castle Point but a little inland.

This change of ownership and location seemed a useful end date for the research. The existence of publications about the Gardens of Troup, by the Banffshire Field Club (Tayler & Tayler, 1937) and the Buchan Field Club (Smith, 1964), supported this view. In addition a date of approximately 1680 had been assigned to Fort Fiddes. However, for reasons set out below, the question of the date of Fort Fiddes re-surfaced from time to time and, ultimately and unexpectedly, was resolved. As this arose from two new strands of evidence, it was essential to include that here. However a detailed history of the Gardens of Troup is outwith the scope of this text.

The second set of contexts which extended the scope of the research is more diffuse, but in many respects of greater interest and significance.

One of the intriguing features of the castle on Cullykhan is that it appears to be nameless in the historical record, although clear references to Troup and the lands of Troup exist. It was natural to explore the extent of such lands, who the neighbours of Troup were at particular times, and the extent to which there was interaction between them and those who lived in the castle. Historical maps and plans added to the limited amount of evidence available, and enhanced knowledge and understanding.

All of this had to be seen against the background of wider events. For the period of occupation of the castle, Scotland was often distinguished not by peace, prosperity and harmony, but by violence, uncertainty and upheavals. Landholdings were not static; change occurred for a multitude of reasons – the need to accommodate more family members, political change, death without heirs, and so on.

How had this impacted on Troup and the people who lived there? In what follows the intention is to set the castle at Cullykhan in the context of events in north-east Scotland, and more widely when necessary, but not to write a wider historical narrative. Appendix 5 provides an edited version of the timeline that was developed to facilitate this.

A further element of activity was prompted by consideration of placenames, work largely undertaken by my wife, Jennifer. No one can see the name 'Cullykhan' and not wonder at its derivation. For this, as with other information about possible boundaries of Troup, much of the detailed information is included in appendices.

The book begins with an exploration of the immediate area of the site. Some may know the main features, but the description and images here may encourage others to visit and explore a beautiful area of coast. A summary of the archaeological findings is included. A guide to what has been learned from Maps, Journals and Castles is next, followed by the main conclusions about Place Names.

All of this sets the background for the historical researches with four chapters on the castle and its occupants. The final chapter sets out the story of Fort Fiddes.

Finally, it was not possible to conduct this research without trying, at times, to augment the historical record with informed consideration of the motives and significance of certain individuals, particularly those central to the story of Cullykhan. Hopefully, any speculation is clearly identified as such. It is in the nature of such research that others, faced with the same collection of limited facts, may well draw different conclusions.

In short, the historical research on the occupancy of the castle on Cullykhan prompted many diversions, not all of which are reported here. As for much of Scotland in the period in question, the written record and archaeological data from possibly related sites, is often tantalizingly incomplete or missing, if it ever existed. As a result, insights into the lives of key individuals are limited. Hopefully the approach taken here augments the information about Troup in ways the reader finds helpful and interesting.

2. THE SITE AND ITS SURROUNDINGS

The significance of location in choosing a place for settlement is not a modern phenomenon. It is a good example of how aspects of human nature have clear echoes over lengthy periods of time. What may vary in different epochs is the significance of particular factors in selecting where to make the, usually large, investment of time and resources to create a place to live.

It is important, in reflecting on location and mobility in the medieval period, to have the sage words of Geoffrey Barrow in mind.

> *The geography of Scotland with its hill ranges, its fast rivers of uncertain temper, its fearful mosses and bogs, its many arms of the sea running far inland, has at all times imposed upon human communication a complex pattern of routes by land and sea.*
>
> *(Barrow, 1984, 58)*

Cullykhan is an excellent example of the importance of the surrounding landscape and features for both the choice of location and the nature of settlement. Whichever way Cullykhan is approached today, the view is spectacular. Arguably, the best approach by road is to come from the

This picture is taken from somewhere between Lion's Head and Cullykhan, looking eastwards. The likely date is the late 1960s. On Cullykhan, excavations on the Knoll and the Iron Age site are visible. The site huts are located on the 'bowling green'. In the distance is part of the village of Pennan and the imposing Pennan Head.

south on the New Pitsligo road towards Pennan along the east side of the Tore of Troup. Troup Head and Pennan Head frame a very Scottish landscape of land, cliffs, sea and sky which is ever changing in the fluctuating weather of the north-east of Scotland. The northern part of this road runs parallel to a historic boundary which has been significant up to relatively recent times. The burn in the Tore of Troup, which enters the sea at Nethermill, separated, at differing historical periods, the lands of the earldom of Buchan to the east from the lands of Troup to the west, the parish of Aberdour from the parish of Gamrie, and the county of Aberdeen from the county of Banff.

When the visitor turns along the track towards Cullykhan from the Gardenstown to New Aberdour road, the vista changes. From the car park at the end there is much to see. The eye is drawn to the beautiful bay and beach, bathing haunts for countless generations as well as a sheltered anchorage (OS, 1868, 70). This is the view on the front cover.

The slope down to the beach reveals the remains of a disused mill, and an old jetty. The end of a natural passage called the Needle's E'e follows a fault line under the headland which emerges at the other side of the headland into the Devil's Kitchen (or Dining Room). This feature has attracted comment on a number of occasions. In the Imperial Gazetteer this,

subterraneous passage, through a peninsula of about 150 yards long from sea to sea, through which a man with difficulty can creep. At the north end of this narrow passage is a cave … The whole is supported by immense columns of rock, is exceeding grand, after a person has crept through the narrow passage.

Another writer who was much impressed by the scenery near Troup Head was Charles Cordiner, minister at St Andrew's Chapel in Banff. His description of the Needle's E'e and Deil's Kitchen is also worth noting.

One large vault passes completely through a point of the promontory. The entrance into it is but like a rent in the mass of rock and leads into a dark and narrow cavern, rugged at first, but gradually swelling into a fine arched roof, terminates in a most spacious dome, open to the sea. (Cordiner, 1780, Letter VIII.)

There are no visible columns in the Deil's Kitchen today, although it is still hugely impressive. This is an area where the landscape formed by the forces of nature has left a lasting impression on visitors over hundreds of years. A number of illustrations throughout the text capture aspects of this, but there is no substitute for visiting and looking.

Looking towards Hell's Lum, a blowhole which goes through the next headland, Lion's Head, from the west end of Cullykhan, near the Knoll.

The second picture looks into Hell's Lum, on a very calm day.

Emerging from the Deil's Kitchen, there is no escaping Hell's Lum, a spectacular blowhole (particularly on a windy day) through Lion's Head, the next headland to the west, which inspires a range of emotions in those who visit it. To quote Francis Douglas in 1782,

Wonderful as you may think it, I had the courage to scramble down near to the brink of this horrid chasm, and have thought myself the better man for it ever since (Douglas, 1782, 290).

This is magnificent coastal scenery to explore and enjoy. It is also a geologist's delight, as noted by Hugh Miller.

The rocks which abound the shore are highly interesting, of stupendous height, and various formations (Pratt, 1858, 177 and 192-6).

It is important to remember that, for much of history, travel by sea could be easier and quicker than travel by land. Stories about smugglers clearly demonstrate the area's attractions for that activity. The bay at Cullykhan provides a good landing place; there are not many such locations along the coast east of Banff. Indeed it is called 'the harbor of Cullycan' in the Statistical Account.

This is a landscape of inspiring contrasts and continuing surprises. For example, from both sides of the headland the existence of a route through the headland is well concealed. While the Devil's Kitchen is one of a number of caves along the coast that are clearly visible from the sea, the existence of the Needle's E'e eludes all but the most persistent observer and explorer. Partly this is because of the alignment of the bay at Cullykhan. An approach from the east would immediately draw the eye to the sheltered, sandy bay, but coming from the west the bay is hidden until you are all but in it, a fact which

Finding the Needle's E'e. This view is taken from the rocks on the south side of Cullykhan Bay, with the beach only partially visible to the left. It would be easy to visit Cullykhan and not realize that this fissure in the rock under the headland is there, and that it goes all the way through.

may be significant in the derivation of the name. Coming from the west, the traveller's eye is drawn much more initially to the Tore of Troup and Pennan Bay. Any maritime traveller, having found Cullykhan Bay, would be very aware that it offered great shelter from the prevailing westerly winds and a safe anchorage.

It is worth emphasizing that the Needle's E'e and Hell's Lum are natural features arising from geological faults. Other fault lines are visible in the neighbourhood, pointing to where future caves are being formed. The faults also give rise to significant slippage. It is clear that in places, both on the Castle Site - on both sides of the headland - and at Fort Fiddes, there has been large-scale cliff erosion; it is still possible to find the occasional piece of stonework from the castle on the beach below. Anyone who excavated on the Castle Site was conscious that part of the kitchen and outbuildings had already gone over the cliff. Correspondingly, on the Lion's Head side, the scanty remains of the cobbled surface strongly suggested that other parts, together with some outbuildings, had also disappeared over the cliff edge. Further, parts of the rampart of Fort Fiddes are closer to the modern edge than at the time of construction. An immense area of collapse can be seen from the summit of Lion's Head.

The cliffs on the west side are steep with a continuing process of slippage and collapse taking place, particularly beside the site of the castle and Fort Fiddes. Pennan Head is in the distance.

Taken from Lion's Head looking SE; note the Devil's Kitchen, evidence of erosion on the cliff and the rock falls below. Pennan can be seen in the distance, and Nethermill at the sea end of the Tore of Troup.

From the car park, the defensive attractions of the promontory as a site for settlement are clear. Arguably, at times the need for a safe haven may have been the primary reason for its choice for habitation. The modern land access is via a narrow path on a bridge over a burn (a man-made water course as a power source for the mill further down, nearer the beach) which runs into the sea in the bay to the east of the headland. The construction of the bridge used stone originally from the castle. The burn would also have

Modern, probably 18th century, access bridge to the promontory, using stone from the castle. The flow of water was channelled to support the mill near the beach.

16

served as a likely water supply for settlements on Cullykhan. It rises on the farm of Northfield on Troup Head, runs parallel to the coast then divides with one branch, known in the Statistical Account as the Water of Troup, running into the sea on either side of Cullykhan. It is easy to see that limiting access to the peninsula from the land would not have been difficult.

Looking NE shows the overall shape of the headland. The surface is level, facilitating its use for habitation. Also note that the remains of the castle are at the narrowest point. Fort Fiddes lies beyond that.

The headland is irregular in outline, approximately 240 metres long with 20 metre high cliffs. It is also fairly level which would have made planning and building easier. This is in marked contrast to neighbouring headlands, such as Lion's Head, where the angle of slope would make construction significantly more difficult. All these headlands 'command sublime views of the ever-changeful ocean to the North', a very apt comment in Groome's Gazetteer.

Although the headland is exposed, it is sheltered in part from weather from the west, and north-west in particular, because it is in the lea of Troup Head. According to Mr Whyte, the Parochial Schoolmaster and author of the chapter on Gamrie in the 1845 Statistical Account.

*the warmest and earliest part of the parish (of Gamrie) is the
eastern or Troup district, which has the double advantage of south
exposure, and of shelter from the north blast by the rocks of Troup
Head.*

In addition to room for habitation, Cullykhan headland is sufficiently
large, approximately 0.6 ha (1.5 acres), to provide space to keep animals
and for a modest level of cultivation. The sea, shore and cliffs are also
potential sources of food. No accounts of what the local people
consumed prior to 1683 have been found. However, the paper by
Alexander Garden of Troup, referred to later in this text, provides a
description which may reflect enduring practice in the area, subject to
climate change.

From the headland there are extensive views up the Tore of Troup,
across to the village of Pennan and further to the east, as well as a fine
open aspect out to sea.

The impression is that this was not a densely populated landscape but
it has been settled for a long time. Travel, even over short distances, is
not straightforward. The manner in which the coast is sharply divided by
Dens (such as Afforsk and Melrose) and the Tore of Troup shows that
routeways through the area would not have been easy to find or traverse.
This fragmentation of the landscape within Gamrie parish can be
illustrated in another way, again by reference to Groome's Gazetteer,

*not a drop of water runs into Gamrie parish from any other parish,
but all its burns either rise within itself or merely touch its
boundaries; several of them are highly interesting for either the
fitfulness of their course, the beauty of their falls, or the utility of
their water power.*

Of course the fact that people live in an area of fine scenery and grand
landscapes does not mean that living is easy. People will have had to
work hard to survive and prosper from the resources of the land and the
sea.

To summarise, the area round Cullykhan is one of the finest settings on
the beautiful Banffshire coast. Troup Head, slightly to the west, is a
dominant landmark which can be seen, often from large distances. On
this stretch of coast east from Banff, there are few places where a boat
could safely be beached. The bay at Cullykhan is arguably the best place
and the associated headland served as a good location for human
settlement from the prehistoric period until modern times.

The Archaeological Context

Prior to the excavation, a number of physical features on the site offered clear clues to periods of use. These included exposed pieces of vitrification along what appeared to be a rampart. Ditches could be seen, and are still visible, at various locations. On what was termed the Castle Site, some substantial lumps of fallen masonry existed; some remnants are still there. Beyond this, a level area said to be a former bowling green was clear, though now it has the main spoil heaps from the excavations on the Castle Site on it. It is still possible to make out the ramparts of Fort Fiddes at the end of the promontory.

The surface of the headland, the sides of the cliffs, and the evidence at the bottom of the cliffs suggest strongly that there has been slippage, perhaps significantly so in some parts. Of particular relevance here is the position of the castle, directly above the Needle's E'e and Devil's Dining Room. As mentioned earlier, this is a geological fault line.

The surface of the headland as it is today, and as it was prior to excavation. Shown here is one of the ditch features on the site. Also visible is a mound of fallen masonry; there were more on the Castle Site prior to excavation. Pennan and Pennan Head are in the distance.

Those wishing to explore the detail of the archaeological excavations and their findings are directed to the reports listed in the Bibliography. For completeness a brief summary is given here.

The earliest evidence pointed to some use of the site in the neolithic period. The earliest phase of construction uncovered was a platform site at the northern side of the promontory, perhaps dating to about 450 BC. This was followed, about 300 BC, by a defensive palisade at the western approach on the Knoll. This was later replaced by a great timber gateway. The remains of a number of oak posts are still in situ in the postholes. This gateway must have been an imposing, possibly also intimidating, sight when in use. It also reflects a compelling need for security and shelter on the part of those who built it.

An impression of how the entrance may have looked.   Drawn by William Lindsay

Inside the gateway, a contemporary industrial area was uncovered which showed evidence of tin, copper and bronze working. Anyone who spends time on Cullykhan will readily testify how a 'draught' could be channeled to enhance combustion. Finds here included a complete crucible for metal-working, remains of industrial waste, furnaces and hearths. Pottery, metal and stone artefacts were also recovered. All of this was on a cobbled surface created by setting beach pebbles in the clay that overlies the headland. Such a surface could be easily repaired. More significantly, it made the difference between a clay surface that, in wet weather, would become a slippery morass and a surface that people could live on more easily.

A timber-laced stone rampart was subsequently constructed but the excavations did not reveal any evidence of contemporary occupation associated with this rampart. The rampart on the north and west sides was destroyed by fire, producing the vitrification mentioned above. The final phase of use in the pre-medieval period was the construction of a number of walls and a U-shaped flat-bottomed ditch. This takes occupation up to the seventh century AD approximately.

A portion of the vitrified west rampart of the fort. The stone has been fused together as a result of the heat generated by fire.

The prehistoric activity covered a relatively small area, showing the complexity of interpreting the range of evidence. Further complications were evident on the Knoll, an even smaller area, as a later, probably late eighteenth century, carriageway had been dug out, damaging some of the early occupations, and the waste from this was dumped on top of the Knoll.

For the periods covered by this historical research, three parts of the headland are relevant. The first is the Knoll where there was a well-established medieval household, with an associated concentration of twelfth century finds, including a coin, gilt buckle plate and pottery, both Scottish and imported. More than one phase of building was noted here. To the west of this was a V-shaped ditch, running in a north-south direction, in which was found twelfth/thirteenth century pottery.

The other major location of construction and occupation in the medieval period was further along the peninsula, at the narrowest point above the passage of the Needle's E'e, where a rectangular stone-built keep was built. Although little remained of this phase of the castle, an impression of how it may have appeared is given by looking at the photos of Old Wick Castle in the next chapter. There was clear evidence for occupation of this castle over a prolonged period. For example, a number

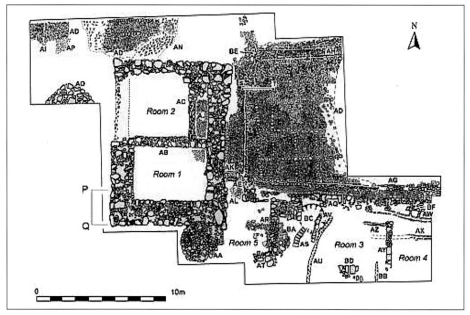

This plan shows the full extent of the excavated area on the Castle Site, as per the published report by Moira Greig. The main features to note are the remains of the foundations of the original rectangular tower and the extensive cobbled courtyard laid out in a grid-like pattern with integral drains. The rooms within the tower were clearly basement rooms floored with natural clay from the headland. More limited remains exist on the south-east where the later kitchen, with the fine collapsed arch, was built over an earlier outbuilding. To the north there are more scanty remains of possible outbuildings. On both sides, the loss of structures due to slippage and collapse can be seen although the full extent of the original buildings can only be a matter of conjecture.

of phases/alterations to the building were identified including a substantial cobbled courtyard to the east, a kitchen and outbuildings.

Within the kitchen was a collapsed fireplace arch bearing two masons' marks. A small quantity of pottery sherds, three coins (dated to the

This wonderful aerial picture was taken in 1971. It shows almost the full extent of the areas excavated over the years of digging, prior to the site being covered again, for protection. The shape of the castle is clearly visible from the remaining foundations, with the proximity to the edge of the cliffs on both sides only too apparent. Also clear is the very narrow access to the site, (in the bottom right hand corner of the photo), a defensive feature for a number of phases of settlement. The largest open excavated area includes the area of late Bronze Age and early Iron Age working. Careful examination of the Knoll, the other significant excavated area in the foreground, shows the excavated postholes where some of the timbers for the gateway were embedded.

sixteenth century), and a few other artefacts were also recovered. Evidence of earlier medieval structures underlay the kitchen area, including a number of stone drains, two narrow clay-lined channels and a pit.

Little of the castle was still in place, the most notable exception being the well-constructed cobbled courtyard. The plan illustrates that even the base course of the wall was not complete. In addition to the collapsed masonry mentioned above, the evidence of slippage showed that a significant proportion of the kitchen had gone over the cliff. A further source of destruction undoubtedly arose in the process of constructing Fort Fiddes; the carriageway mentioned in relation to the Knoll continued through the Castle Site to Fort Fiddes.

The finds support the view that the likely dates for this occupation stretch from the thirteenth to the seventeenth century. Trying to match the historical and archaeological data for the castle was a recurring theme of the research.

Finally, the construction of Fort Fiddes also became a matter of research, although it was not the subject of major excavation. Later estate maps show that the headland was used for grazing animals and perhaps some cultivation, which may explain why the area inside the ramparts of the vitrified fort was devoid of coherent evidence of occupation.

The range of use, both in terms of time and purpose, of this comparatively small headland still seems amazing. While the concentration in this publication will be on the historical elements, it is certain that, in archaeological terms, Cullykhan is more likely to be remembered for its prehistoric archaeology, for example the metal working.

A further question, repeatedly prompted by this place, is how many other headlands along this coast would reveal the same exciting and illuminating range of evidence about our ancestors if they were fully explored and excavated. Given the significance of travel by sea, and its relative ease compared to land travel, it is possible many other promontories along this coast have castles with earlier undiscovered occupation associated with them.

3. MAPS, JOURNALS AND CASTLES

This chapter brings together three strands of my research. Looking for informative maps and plans about the area was an ongoing activity. The castle at Cullykhan was not unknown to early map-makers. The occasional journal entry relating to the site was a welcome discovery and these are included below; other journal or diary entries are included at appropriate points in the text. The information about other castles seemed to mount inexorably – in terms of chronology, building features and location – with the challenge being to seek relevance to Troup and, more widely, some order within it.

Maps

Timothy Pont's map of the area shows a castle at Troup. Jan Jannsen's map, *Scotland between the River Tay and the Moray Firth* published in

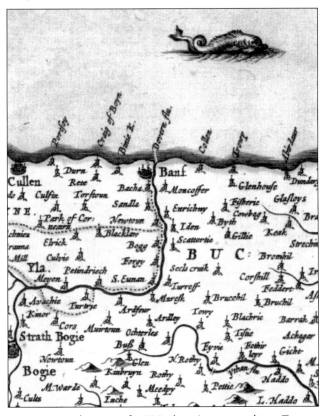

Amsterdam in 1659, also shows a castle at Troup, among a number of castles along the coast. Robert Gordon's map, published by Blaeu in Amsterdam in 1654, also indicates Troup, and other places which feature in this narrative. A similar pattern shows in the 'corrected and improved' version of Gordon's map published by Robert Morden in London in 1687. Morden published a very similar map, again indicating Troup, in London in 1695. A

Jan Jannsen's map of 1659 showing a castle at Troup.

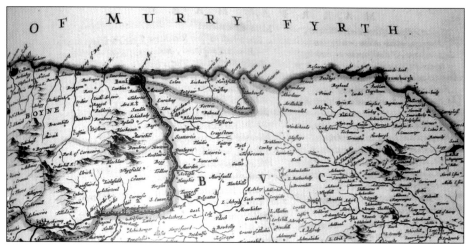

Gordon's map shows Troup and other castles along the Banffshire coast. Note Lichnot, Northfield, Colen and Gamrie Kirk, which all feature in the research.

map of Scotland by Nicolaus Visscher, published in Amsterdam in 1689, includes Troup among places in the area such as 'Gemrie, Linchnoth, Colen and Doun'. These examples support the view that settlement was known at Troup, that there was a castle there and that it should be called the castle of Troup.

However, it should be noted that not all maps in this period show a castle at Troup, which is puzzling. A number of maps have a place designated Tyer to the east of Banff, sometimes with a castle symbol. Examples of this include Mercator's map of 1595, published in Duisberg, which is based on an earlier map of 1573 by Ortelius. Two later maps by Hendrick Hondius (Amsterdam, 1636) and Vincenzo Coronelli (Venice, 1696) are very similar to Mercator's map and show Tyer on an inlet on the coast between Banff and Aberdour.

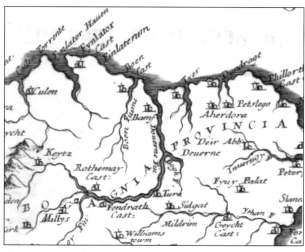

Extract from Coronelli's map (1696) showing Tyer.

Two possible explanations can be put forward. First, it is possible that this is a reference to Tyrie. It was probably known as the site of a motte, destroyed in the first half of the nineteenth century as part of land improvements, and is said to be near a site where the Danes had been defeated (Groome, 1882, Vol VI, 484). However, Tyrie is well inland and considerably further east than these maps indicate; in short, the marked position could be wrong. The features mentioned above – motte, battle with Danes – also fit other locations, such as Gamrie. A further possibility is that, based on Gordon of Straloch's notes, Towy (as in the Barclays of Towie whose castle was at Colen or Cullen to the west of Troup) was interpreted as Tyer by a later scribe (Gordon, 1908, 278). Alternatively, it may be that Tyer is also Troup.

A fine estate map (Archives of the University of Aberdeen, MS2626) prepared by John Home in 1767 shows clearly that the promontory was designated Castle Hill but does not indicate any remains. Later maps do not necessarily use the name Castle Point, but do identify Fort Fiddes or Fiddies. This applies to the map by Robertson in 1822 of Aberdeen, Banff and Kincardine and to the 1826 map by John Thomson in his Atlas of Scotland.

In considering these maps, it is interesting to note the places which are named in some maps but not others, particularly when such names do not feature on more modern maps.

A plan attributed to John Ray said to be produced in 1707 has previously been published. The status and content of this plan is considered in Chapter 9 on Fort Fiddes.

A full list of the maps and plans consulted is given in Appendix 4.

Travellers' Journals

Some references to the scenic features of the area were included in the previous chapter. However, information about the site in journals is limited; perhaps the coastal scenery was too much of a distraction.

Robert Gordon of Straloch, in preparing the map of the area mentioned above, described some castles along the coast, noting that 'Next comes Troup, built (at the sea) on an isthmus, now deserted' (Gordon, 1908, 278). Unfortunately Gordon's Journal can only be dated with certainty to the range 1608-61; a date around 1640, when the description of Moray was written (Rhind, 1839, 3) is perhaps most likely. There is no clear evidence, archaeological or historical, of when the castle was abandoned. A more precise date for Gordon's note would be extremely helpful.

In 1722 William Duncan simply states that there is an old castle at Troup (Duncan, 1908, 48). In 1777 Williams, who was more interested in the vitrification evident on the Iron Age Site, mentions that 'there are some very obscure ruins of stone and lime work, which appear to have been very strong' on Cullykhan (Williams, 1777, 67). Finally, the Ordnance Survey Name Book for Banffshire in 1868 records that on the same promontory as Fort Fiddes faint traces of the foundation walls of an ancient stronghold or castle are to be seen.

These pieces of evidence, together with location, and the maps mentioned earlier, support the conclusion that the castle on Cullykhan was called Troup Castle.

Castles

Scotland is rich in terms of the number of castles it has, and had. A great deal is known about a few of these, through records and excavation. However, information about many of them, including Troup, is absent, although that has not prevented writers ascribing dates and people to them.

The absence of information about Troup was the main impetus for pursuing a range of comparisons in the hope that some insights about Troup would follow. In no order of priority, the comparative themes can be summarized as location, people & families, known timeframe, excavation, and building features. There is some reference to this in the published report on the castle by Moira Greig.

Perhaps the most distinctive feature of the castle on Cullykhan is its location on a coastal promontory that could be readily defended. A number of other castles along the Banffshire and Aberdeenshire coastline are similarly situated. Dundarg Castle, to the east of New Aberdour and one of the seats of the Comyns, is a striking example. Craig o' Boyne Castle, between Portsoy and Whitehills, and Findlater Castle, between Sandend and Cullen, also enjoy spectacular clifftop locations.

The Comyns were known as great builders. Looking beyond the north-east of Scotland, two particular examples of Comyn castles seemed of potential interest – Cruggleton Castle in Galloway and Tarset in Northumberland, both of which have some documentary and excavation evidence.

Other inhabitants of the Scottish coastline identified the need for fortified living spaces. Examples exist along the coast from Caithness to Easter Ross, such as Old Wick, Forss and Redcastle. Any study of historic maps, such as Blaeu's Atlas, shows a large number of promontory castles on the coast between Fraserburgh and Wick. The illustrations of Old Wick illuminate a similar setting and may also convey the style of building of the casle on Cullykhan, albeit using a very different stone.

Site and remains of Findlater Castle, between Sandend and Cullen.

These examples raise some questions. Did the Comyns influence the plans for castle construction along the coast, up to, say, their defeat by Robert Bruce in 1308? Did the movement of people from Tynedale, where there were landholdings both of David I (before he became King) and the Comyns, transplant people who had experience in castle building to the north-east of Scotland? Were there links across the Moray Firth, reflected in the style of, say, Old Wick and Cullykhan? One of the significant features of Cullykhan is that it was a settlement used in earlier times. For how many other promontory sites is that true, and is it an important pointer? In all these considerations, the relative ease or difficulty of travel by land or sea is a recurring theme.

The remains of Old Wick on the Caithness coast, from which the Banffshire coast is visible on a clear day, illustrate how a promontory location was used and the style of the original tower. The castle at Troup may have been similar in terms of thickness of walls and access.

This picture probably dates to 1971. It is taken looking back towards the car park from the main spoil heap for the Castle Site. The main feature is the area of cobbling with the main drain running through it. The main digging activity is on the kitchen area of the site, only part of which is revealed at this stage. The limited remains of the castle foundations can also be seen. The quality of the drain may be the best testimony of the need to draw water off for storage and to keep the underfoot conditions more habitable.

In addition to location, some other features of the castle on Cullykhan were striking. In particular, the quality of the cobbled courtyard - set out in a pattern of stones, with fine drains - matched, and perhaps exceeded, the quality, if not the extent, of those at Kildrummy Castle or Balvenie Castle. Is this significant?

The fireplace arch from the kitchen had parallels at Edzell Castle. The search for other locations of the distinctive mason's

Part of the cobbled courtyard at Kildrummy Castle.

mark on the arch was lengthy but did yield results which may assist in dating that phase of the castle (see Chapter 8 on Keiths). It also sparked a major and ongoing initiative by Moira Greig on recording and documenting masons' marks in historic buildings; a project that should have been undertaken in Scotland earlier.

Other castles with potential similarities included Hallforest, in terms of style of construction and dating, and Dunnideer, with a link to the Balliols. Sadly, for some castles where comparison would have been of great interest, for example Colen of the Barclays, all evidence has been lost. The published reports on Dundarg Castle were examined but, like others, the limited remains of the castle at Cullykhan constrain the ability to draw meaningful conclusions.

Some of these thoughts are incorporated into the narrative which follows. However, the lingering impression is that not enough is known about most Scottish castles to move beyond possible connections of the types considered here to firmer conclusions. Put another way, there remains great scope for research to illustrate questions such as:

- Which castles were occupied at the same time?
- How many castles sit above earlier habitation sites?
- Why did some castles endure and some were more transient?
- How many people might have lived in each one?
- Why were so many built on headlands where access was – is – challenging?
- Can we achieve a better match between known historic trends and events and the patterns of castle construction and occupation? How does this vary across Scotland?

The excavation and research done on Troup can only provide limited insight into such questions. The conclusion which had to be drawn, at times reluctantly, was that to complete the work on Troup, these fascinating questions would have to be set aside.

Perhaps the above provides food for thought for others to take forward.

4. PLACE NAME EVIDENCE

The research undertaken by Jennifer McKay on place names in the area has a number of strands. The first looks at the names Troup and Cullykhan, whose importance is self-evident. The second strand encompasses names which are mentioned in the story, such as Crovie, Lethnot, Melrose. A third strand looks at names, such as farm names, on the lands of Troup. Finally, consideration is given to the names associated with coastal features.

Troup

The Troup name is a mystery. Toponomists, place-name experts, seem to have given this name a wide berth. In his seminal work of 1926, *The History of the Celtic Place Names of Scotland*, W J Watson, although mentioning the name in the passing, does not address the question of its meaning. The inference that one draws is that Watson did not believe it was a Celtic name, that is, not Gaelic.

Place-name scholars search the written record, legal documents such as wills and charters, for the names they are investigating; they are looking specifically for early references, the earlier the better. Working with an early form of a name increases the chance of getting close to the original meaning. In Troup, we are fortunate to have a very early date. In a charter written sometime between the years 1189 and 1198, King William the Lion granted the 'ecclesiam de Gamerin et capella de trub', the 'church of Gamerin and the chapel of trub', to the monks of his new Abbey at Arbroath.

It is, therefore, beyond doubt that the name Troup has an extremely old pedigree. As described earlier, archaeological excavations have uncovered evidence of human activity on Cullykhan from the Neolithic through the Bronze Age and the Iron Age, long before English or Gaelic were spoken here. Pictish was spoken before Gaelic speakers arrived from the ninth century (Nicolaisen, 1999, 67-82).

In the absence of any plausible interpretations of the Troup name, from experts or others, I offer the following hypothesis. There was an Old Gaelic word **treb** which may have been related to an earlier Pictish word which place name scholars believe meant a 'farm, land-holding' (Taylor, S, 2012,

195). As vowel sounds change with usage and the passage of time, it is perfectly possible that **treb** would have evolved into trub. [b] and [p] are the same sound, the difference being that [b] is voiced and [p] is unvoiced and so trub would quite naturally become Troup, voiced consonants tending to lose their voiced quality with prolonged use.

Another medieval spelling of Troup was Trop. There is a very old Swedish word **torp** meaning 'village' or a 'small settlement' (Geoffrey Issott, pers. comm.). The transposition of letters (metathesis) in the evolution of words over time is a common occurrence, particularly in the case of 'r' and a vowel. This perhaps suggests an ancient root for the Troup name and may shed a glimmer of light on the language spoken here in antiquity.

Cullykhan

On Ordnance Survey maps, the name Cullykhan denotes only the bay and the beach, as in Cullykhan Bay and Cullykhan Shore. The First Edition Ordnance Survey, 6 inch to the mile, map published in 1869 calls the headland Castle Point and all subsequent maps bear this name. Locally, however, the name of the headland is, unequivocally, Cullykhan.

We can be confident that the second part of the name, 'khan', is a version of the Gaelic **ceann** which means a 'head' or 'end point' (Simon Taylor, pers. Comm.). In *Scottish Place-names No 37*, Carole Hough makes the point that "The head in both Gaelic (ceann) and Scots (heid) can designate the top of a vertical feature or the end of a horizontal one (Hough, C, 2014, 6). In modern place names **ceann** often occurs in the anglicized form 'kin' as in Kinloch, Kintyre, Kincardine and so on.

The meaning of the first part of the name is less clear cut. It may derive from the Gaelic **coille** meaning 'a wood' or the Gaelic **cuil** a 'corner or hidden spot', or indeed from the Gaelic **cul** meaning 'at the back of'. Without doubt, the name Cullykhan is of Gaelic origin.

It may seem strange to learn that a place name, in an area as immersed in the Doric as Gamrie, should be of Gaelic origin but Gaelic was spoken on the Buchan coast for several hundred years, from the ninth century until as late as the thirteenth century and possibly even longer (Nicolaisen, 1999, 67-82).

In Gaelic place names there is a general, though not infallible, rule that the first element of a name is a reference to a topographical feature such as valley, cliff, confluence, cave, field, ford etc. and the second element is a qualifier, for example, big, small, black, green, high up, water-logged or the name of a person associated with the place, names of flora or fauna associated with the place or some allusion to folk memories of the place. If this logic is applied to Cullykhan, then the first element is the feature in the landscape i.e. the wood or the hidden corner or the area at the back of somewhere. The second part is describing this element, giving us information to differentiate it from other similar features.

Cullykhan appears to mean something along the lines of 'the hidden neuk at the end point' or perhaps, 'the place behind the end point'; the meaning depends on the derivation: **cuil** or **cul**. If we accept that the name applies only to the bay, the shore and the slope up to the modern car park,

This view, taken from out at sea, shows the beach and foreshore at Cullykhan. The headland goes off on the right. The area in the centre of the picture may be the first named Cullykhan; it is undoubtedly a sheltered, almost hidden, neuk. The line of the burn down to the beach can be seen; on the lower slope, just above the stony part of the beach, is the site of the former mill.

the former derivation is certainly an accurate description of the Cullykhan shore area.

This interpretation does not sit entirely comfortably with the fact that the headland is also known as Cullykhan. Perhaps the headland acquired this name by association with, and its close proximity to, the 'hidden neuk'.

This could have happened when non-Gaelic-speaking people, who did not understand the meaning of the name, settled in the area.

This is the Tore of Troup as it nears the sea at Nethermill. The burn is the historic boundary, mentioned at several places in the text, between the parish of Gamrie and the parish of Aberdour, the earldom of Buchan and the lands of Troup, and historic Banffshire and Aberdeenshire.

Cullykhan is close to the end of the Tore of Troup. As mentioned earlier, the burn in the Tore is a longstanding and significant dividing line which may have been a boundary prior to parishes having been created. Perhaps Cullykhan is the 'hidden neuk' at the end of an ancient administrative entity or the end point of a boundary between land holdings.

Given that Gaelic place names are so intimately connected to topography, our most persuasive evidence must come from observation of the landscape rather than the written record. All the more so in the case of Cullykhan as, unlike Troup, there is no mention of the name Cullykhan in any existing early charters.

Maps can sometimes offer clues. The oldest maps of the area are the Pont map of the last decade of the sixteenth century and Gordon of

Straloch's map, largely based on Pont's work, printed in Blaeu's *Atlas Novus of 1654.*

The name Cullykhan appears on neither of those maps. The maps depict settlements and significant buildings; names of physical features are largely absent. This could suggest that there were no buildings at that time with the name Cullykhan. However, it is apparent from charter evidence that named farms, which do not feature on Pont's map, existed before his map was drawn. Clearly, Pont and Gordon made decisions to leave certain information off their maps. These maps do not show the Cullykhan peninsula or neighbouring Lion's Head; they are subsumed into one amorphous, ill-defined mass along with Troup Head which would appear, from the lack of definition, not to have been surveyed by Pont or Gordon.

It is perhaps odd that Gordon did not provide more detail as it is likely that he would have been familiar with the area as he held the teinds (income which, before the Reformation, was given to the Church) of Troup for a period up to 1654. However, the information he included on his map would have been predicated on the purpose for which the map was prepared.

The earliest written record of the name found to date is an entry in the Gamrie parish baptismal records for September 1721 where listed among witnesses is "Marjory Robertson Spous to William Moreson miln of Cullicane". The mill was situated on the slope above the beach, not on the headland, although very close to it.

The first appearance of the name on an existing drawing is on the estate plan of 1767, prepared by surveyor, John Home for Garden of Troup at the time of the agricultural improvements. This plan shows us 'Cullican', apparently a group of buildings, perhaps a farm, in the general area of the site of the modern car park above the beach. The mill, closer to the headland is also marked.

In June 1785, the miller, James Morrison, wrote from 'Culy Can' to Lord Gardenstone asking for the renewal of his lease. In the letter Mr Morrison reminds Lord Gardenstone that his grandmother had cured his lordship of the jaundice when he was small boy and that Lord Gardenstone's grateful grandfather had promised the Morrison family the lease in perpetuity.

The report in *The Scots Magazine* of March 1804 (see chapter on Fort Fiddes) refers to the headland as 'Coulie-cann, or Castlehill'. This is the only written reference the author has seen which clearly names the headland as Cullykhan.

Estate accounts for 1849 record the payment of 10/- to Charles West for a boat from Pennan Quarry to 'Culycan'.

The first edition OS map of 1869 displays the first appearance of the spelling 'Cullykhan'. Where did this new spelling come from? Ordnance Survey recorders diligently followed a protocol when collecting information to be included on their maps. They would ask a minimum of two 'reliable' local informants to name features in the landscape and to confirm their spelling. This information was recorded in the Ordnance Survey Name Book for the parish. In the case of Cullykhan their primary informant was the landowner, F W Garden Campbell Esq. of Troup. He provided the 'Cullykhan' version, despite the spelling 'Culycan' having appeared in his estate accounts less than twenty years earlier. One can but surmise that Garden Campbell invented the new spelling with its rather oriental look.

The Ordnance Survey also enquired of two local men: William Johnstone, a fisherman in his late sixties, resident in Crovie and Thomas Smith of Pennan. Both these gentlemen agreed that 'Cullykhan' was the usual spelling. It is possible, however, that they had never seen the word in writing and as this was the spelling provided by the laird, they simply agreed with his version. He owned the land; he could spell the names on it in any way he chose.

The Name Book record is as follows.

> *Cullykhan Bay: a small bay or creek on the coast, at the extreme east end of the parish of Gamrie, used by F W G Campbell as anchorage for his yacht.*

With his choice of the words, 'the extreme east end of the parish', the OS recorder has picked up on the significant position of Cullykhan which may have given it its name.

Cullykhan was a place of human activity long before the Gaelic language reached this part of Scotland, at the very earliest, in the seventh century AD. Consequently, it could not have been called Cullykhan before then. The prehistoric settlement must surely have had a Pictish name and perhaps an even earlier pre-Celtic name. Cullykhan may be a translation of an earlier name or perhaps it was coined by the Gaelic-speaking incomers. We will never know. What we do know is that Cullykhan is a name belonging to the North East's Gaelic speaking era and is probably more than a thousand years old.

Gaelic Origin Names

Cullykhan and several names in its vicinity have survived the disappearance of Gaelic in the northeast of Scotland and its replacement by Scots English. Other names nearby which are of Gaelic origin are: Crovie, Lichnet, Auchmedden, Findon, Afforsk and Melrose.

Received wisdom is that Crovie means 'at the place of the tree' from the Gaelic **croabh**, 'tree'. However, there is another possibility. The Gaelic **crobh**, a 'hand or paw' used in a topographical context to mean a 'hollow or depression' (Taylor, 2012, 187) may be a more likely interpretation. Immediately above the village of Crovie and adjacent to the farm of Crovie, there is a large depression in the slope which looks like the result of a major landslip. Such a landmark could well have provided the origin of the name. This depression is now marked on maps as 'Corbie Brae'. This suggests an association with crows, **corbie** being the Scots for 'crow' but it is as likely to be an example of metathesis whereby the 'o' and the 'r'

View of the village of Crovie from the path from Gardenstown. The 'hollow or depression', highlighted in the text, is a clear feature above the village houses.

have changed places. Another possibility is that is reflects an earlier spelling of Crovie.

The earliest written records of Crovie are from 1413 charters. These, of course, refer to the farm; the fishing village, it is usually claimed, dates from the eighteenth century and was called after the farm. In the earliest of these charters, the earl Marischal reserved superiority of 'Curvi' and in another, the Duke of Albany confirmed a grant of 'Curvie' to the Barony of Troup. The estate plan of 1767 has 'Crovie'. Taylor and Skinner's Survey of maps of roads of 1776 uses the spelling 'Crevie'.

Lichnet has a history of many variations in spelling: Lethenot (1226), Lechnocht (1500), Lichnot (1654), Lightnet (1767) and Lightnot (1869). In the usual Gaelic name pattern, the first element, the landscape feature, **leth** means a 'slope' and the second element means 'bare, exposed, cold'. This is an appropriate name for land exposed to north-westerly winter gales.

Auchmeddan or Auchmedden are the only versions of the name over the centuries. 'Auch' is 'field' deriving from the Gaelic **achadh** and 'meddan' is likely to be an anglicised version of **meadhan**, meaning 'middle'.

Findon is likely to mean the 'white fort'.

Afforsk, in Taylor and Skinner's Roads Survey of 1776, is 'Auchorsk' and the name appears again, in a bond giving surety for a sum borrowed by Garden of Troup in 1792, as 'Auquhorsk'. The first element derives from **achadh** the Gaelic for 'field' which is often anglicised in modern names as 'auch' or 'ach'. The second element is likely to derive from the Gaelic **chroisg** for 'crossing'. We can compare this name to Afforsk in the Garioch. In 1391 it was 'Achqwhorsk' which according to W J Watson (1926, 486) means 'field of the crossing' from the Gaelic **Achadh a' Chroisg**. Another Watson, Angus, in his unpublished PhD thesis (Watson, 2002, 66) asserts that **chroisg** refers to routes which cross over a watershed. This definition accords well with the situation of Afforsk in Gamrie which straddles the high ground between the Dens of Afforsk and Findon, both with water courses running through them.

Finally, Melrose which in 1385 was 'Melros', 1528 'Mailros' and 1654 'Maillers', before reverting to 'Mellrose' by 1822. W J Watson (1926, 496) has it that the Gaelic **ros** is a 'thing forestanding', a 'projection' and hence

The Den of Afforsk (to the right) and the Den of Findon (to the left).

a 'promontory'. This writer would, however, argue that the 'thing forestanding' is as likely to be any feature prominent in the landscape and would accurately describe Melrose Law, a prehistoric burial cairn which stands conspicuously on the skyline. The first element, contrary to the usual formula, is the qualifier; it derives from the Gaelic **maol** meaning 'bare' or 'blunt'. 'Melrose' is a Gaelic description of a prominent rounded landscape feature and the Scots word 'law' can mean a rounded, often conical hill, thus giving us an example of linguistic redundancy whereby a feature is described identically or similarly in two languages simultaneously. This phenomenon tends to manifest itself on the arrival

Melrose Law, seen from the south west

of a new group of people speaking a different language from the indigenous settled population. In this case it seems that Scots-English speakers, not knowing the meaning of 'Melrose' added an unnecessary 'law' to the name. It seems reasonable to suppose that the estate of Melrose took its name from this eye-catching burial cairn.

Nearby Pennan's name may be Pictish. It should be borne in mind that the name originates in the farm of Pennan, on the headland above the village. The fishing village was referred to as 'Shore of Auchmedden' in early charters. Pictish and Gaelic belonged to the Celtic group of languages and were loosely related. It is thought that the Pictish element **pen** is equivalent to the Gaelic **ceann**, meaning 'head' or 'end point'. The **an** added to the end of **pen** is possibly a diminutive suffix which suggests the name may mean 'small or low head'. Pennan Head is certainly lower than the nearby Troup Head. Not much further to the west is Gamrie Head, sometimes called More Head, **more** meaning 'big' in Gaelic, the highest point on the southern shore of the Moray Firth. Name-givers may have consciously drawn a comparison between the relative heights of the headlands.

Pennan lies in the parish of Aberdour. Aberdour is a rare example of a wholly Pictish place name. **Aber** is Pictish for 'confluence' and **dour** means 'water'. Aberdour, the site of the ancient St Drostan's Church and St Drostan's Well, is where the Dour Burn enters the sea.

Language and Landscape

In the area around Troup there are three strands of language evident in the place names. There are hints of Pictish, several clear examples of Gaelic and an overlay of Scots and English.

It is not known when Scots-English names first appeared in Buchan but anglicisation would have started from the time of the ecclesiastical expansion and the planting of English-speaking monks initiated by David I from the mid twelfth century. We do not know how long the transition from Gaelic to Scots took but it is likely to have taken several generations. The earliest written examples of Scots-English place names in our area are farm names. There is mention in a charter of 'Northfield' being separated from the Lands of Troup in 1462; this may have been a new name or a well-established name.

The dominant features in the coastal landscape: More Head, Crovie Head, Troup Head, Cullykhan and Pennan Head are ancient names; names given by speakers of Pictish or Gaelic who would have used these features as navigational marks in their travels by land or sea. Cullykhan, when approached and seen from the sea, is an unmistakable 'hidden neuk'. More Head is quite clearly the highest headland on the coast. These names have stood the test of time thanks to their significance in the coastal landscape.

The Pictish or Gaelic speakers who named these headlands may have given smaller rocks and skerries names as well. If they fished the inshore waters, they would have needed names for the rocks in order to be able to speak about them; to warn of dangers; to describe places to find certain fish and so on. If they did give the rocks and caves names, some of these have been lost or partially lost. However, the smaller rocks, wave-cut platforms, points and caves may not have been given names by the Gaelic speaking people if they did not fish along this coast. I would suggest that when fishing became a commercial enterprise pursued by full-time fishermen, from the early eighteenth century, Scots speakers who were drawn into this work from other areas gave the individual rocks and reefs names. Most of the names now in use, being mainly Scots, may have been given in at that time. More detail on farm names and coastal features are given in Appendix 3.

The investigation of the names on and around the Lands of Troup has not shed any specific light on the history of the castle but it has underlined the long history of human activity in the area. It is possible that the ancient name of Troup evolved from a pre-Gaelic word, indicating, perhaps, an unbroken human association with the Cullykhan headland from the earliest days of settlement in north east Scotland.

If the name 'Troup' does, in fact, derive from a pre-Gaelic root, then the name 'Cullykhan' is a more modern name. As it is Gaelic it can only have been in use since the seventh century AD at the very earliest.

The name of Troup still survives in Troup Head and in the farm of Mains of Troup. The name Cullykhan is nowadays very much associated with the beach. Cullykhan is the local name for the headland and is holding its own in local usage and folk memory.

5. EARLIEST HISTORICAL REFERENCES

Introduction

Early historical references in Scotland are often scanty, lacking in context, and not securely dated. All of this applies to Troup. However that does not preclude meaningful consideration of a range of issues. The wider historical record in Buchan and Moray can illuminate events, and help define more likely explanations of events concerning Troup. It is helpful too that David I and William I were active in the north-east in the twelfth century.

After looking at the earliest reference, to Lethnot, this chapter will consider the establishment of Troup, dates and who may have been associated with the landholding. This is also an appropriate point to relate what was happening in the surrounding area.

Lethnot

The earliest reference to lands at Troup concerns Lethnot (sometimes Lichnot, Lethenoth), which is described as three oxgangs lying by the sea between the church of Gamrie and Troup. The church here is St John's Church founded in 1004, now a ruin, on More Head to the west of modern Gardenstown. The reference states that Lethnot was given to the monks of Kinloss Abbey in Moray by Robert Corbet (Ferrerii, 1839, 77) but the date is not specified.

There are a number of later references to the land at Lethnot. For example, the grant was confirmed by William the Lion about 1190 and further confirmed by Alexander II in February 1226 as three bovates of land between the church of Gamrie and Troup (Spalding Club, 1843, 490). There is also mention of this grant in the records of the Bishop of Aberdeen. A reference in 1500 indicates that the rental of the 'villae de Lechnocht' was valued at six merks yearly (Spalding Club, 1847, 365). Lethnot appears to have remained as part of the Abbey lands until the sixteenth century and the distribution of church estates subsequent to the Reformation.

This brief outline prompts many questions.

What can be said about the extent of Lethnot? Who was Robert Corbet? When did the original grant take place? What might this tell us about the lands of Troup and settlement there, particularly the position of Lethnot in relation to other known features?

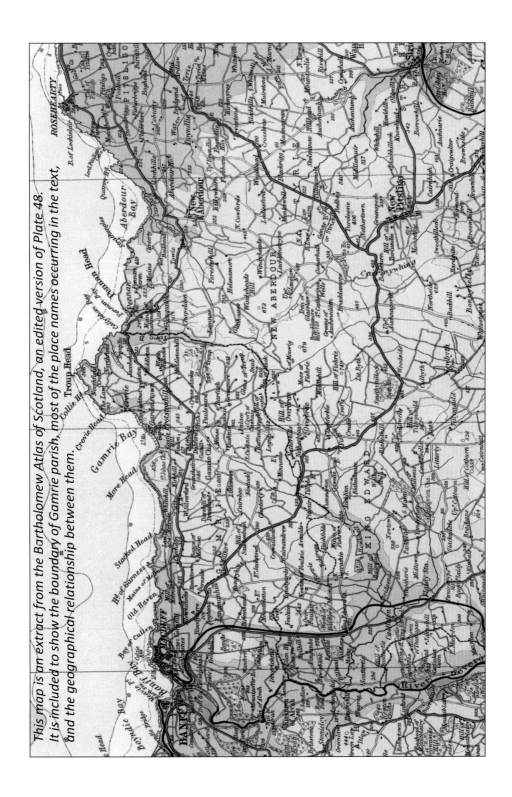

This map is an extract from the Bartholomew Atlas of Scotland, an edited version of Plate 48. It is included to show the boundary of Gamrie parish, most of the place names occurring in the text, and the geographical relationship between them.

45

For the first of these questions, some insight into the extent of Lethnot comes from two events in the sixteenth century. First, in 1518, the Records of the Abbey of Kinloss contain a charter in which Patrick Cheyne of Essilmonth is given use of the lands of Lethnot by Kinloss Abbey (Spalding Club, 1847, 237).

In 1537 there was a court case for the "serveing of ane breve of perambulacion" between Patrick Cheyne "fewar and proprietor of the landis of Lethnot", and Robert abbot of Kinloss "his superior" on the one hand and Gilbert Keith of Troup and the "nobill and mychty lord William erle Merchell his superior" on the other part. In the course of this case, abbot Robert produced a charter of May 1319 (Spalding Club, 1847, 366), to support his claim that Lethnot had been duly assigned to the Abbey. This appears to have clinched the argument; the judgement favoured Cheyne and the abbot of Kinloss. Helpfully, the account of the case gives a description of the march or boundary of Lethnot, the details of which are in Appendix 1.

The likeliest extent of the lands of Lethnot is described in Appendix 1. This photo was taken from the sea looking south. The village of Crovie is the main modern feature. The den or howe running inland from the coast and to the right is part of Lethnot or Lichnet. This is the land granted by Robert Corbet to Kinloss Abbey.

This evidence strongly suggests that the lands of Lethnot were held continuously by Kinloss Abbey and were unaltered from the time of the original grant by Robert Corbet through to the final involvement of Kinloss

Abbey in 1579 when the lands were confirmed to Patrick Cheyne. It appears that Lethnot was a defined area surrounded by other lands in Troup. The names Gilbert Keith, Patrick Cheyne and earl Marischal will figure later in the story.

Wider Context in Twelfth Century Buchan and Moray

To begin to answer the other questions arising from the initial grant of the lands of Lethnot it is necessary to explore what was happening more widely in Buchan and Moray about this time.

What is a Bovate or Oxgang?

Endeavouring a precise definition in terms of modern measurements for medieval – or earlier – measurements is not straightforward, but an understanding of such detail is very useful, for example when considering what a particular landholding might be on the ground. The difficulty is compounded as similar terminology could have differing meanings in different parts of the country, often reflecting the linguistic, cultural and political background when land divisions were established.

Conceptually there could be differences too. By way of illustration, some land measures were framed in terms of how much land could be ploughed/worked by a team of oxen in a particular time. Some appear to be based on the volume of produce, whether cattle or grain, from a piece of land. The same name could be used in both contexts.

Apart from these fundamental differences in approach, other practical factors, such as topography, quality of the soil, the design and effectiveness of the plough used, undoubtedly gave rise to variations, not to mention disputes. One implication of this is the importance of well defined marches between landholdings, and effectively rules for 'common' areas is obvious. In short, the meaning of a specific term was subject to significant variation. For those wishing more detail on the background, further reading specific to this topic is listed in the Bibiliography.

For current purposes, the question is what area does a bovate represent in Troup? As indicated, a bovate – also termed an oxgang or oxgate – could vary, perhaps from 10 to 20 acres. Of course, a Scottish acre was not the same as an English acre being approximately 6150 square (English) yards. The consensus appears to be that, at the time under consideration here, 13 acres approximately would constitute 1 oxgang or bovate, with 8 oxgangs making 1 ploughgate.

In the twelfth century the lands of Buchan were still controlled by Gaelic mormaers, the last of whom was Fergus. The Comyns did not enter the picture until early in the thirteenth century. Generally in this period Buchan, whose western boundary is generally accepted as being the eastern boundary of Troup, is regarded as an area of relative stability. The same can not be said further west where Moray posed a regular and serious threat in the twelfth century (Young, 1993, 175). David I made efforts to impose royal authority in the north. He defeated and killed Angus, last of the Celtic earls of Moray, at Stracathro in 1130 (Duncan, 1989, 166) although this did not presage immediate peace; there were several more years of fighting. Around this time, too, in addition to Flemish colonisation of Moray, a string of royal castles and burghs, stretching from Aberdeen to Inverness, including Banff, was developed along with the reorganisation or development of bishoprics in Aberdeen, Moray, Ross and Caithness.

Excerpt from a manuscript showing David I

Kinloss Abbey was founded in May 1150 by Cistercians from Melrose Abbey. As the northernmost royal foundation of any religious order in Scotland, Kinloss was far removed from the other Cistercian monasteries. While acknowledging David I's pious motives, Oram asserts that Kinloss was as much a political as a religious symbol (Oram, 2004, 197). It was an important part of David I's strategy for pacifying Moray. David would also have been mindful of Norwegian activity emanating from Orkney, exemplified by the raiding of the Norwegian fleet down the east coast, including the sack of Aberdeen, in 1151. The Norwegian threat would strengthen the case for more fortified sites along the coast of Buchan and Moray. Kinloss was supported, particularly in terms of its land holdings, by David's grandson, King William. The extent of land allocated to it established Kinloss Abbey as the greatest monastery in the region (Oram, 2016, 20).

When account is taken of those who were with David I in 1150/1 when he was in Moray and Aberdeen, Oram suggests that the King was undertaking a 'radical reconstruction of arrangements for the future policing of the northern part of the kingdom.' Against this background a redefinition or reallocation of lands such as Troup in the mid-twelfth century would not be surprising. Indeed there may have been a compelling political/military logic as it has also been suggested that Banff thanages, such as Glendowachy immediately to the west of Troup, look like a possible bulwark against the great earldom of Moray (Grant, 1993, 45). David was very conscious of the ongoing potential threat posed by certain families with Moray connections. This would support the view that he would have wished areas such as Troup to be under the control of people he knew and whose loyalty was not in question.

It is also noteworthy that Kinloss Abbey supported the colony in Buchan at Deer Abbey, originally founded by William Comyn, earl of Buchan, from the early years of the thirteenth century.

The remains of Kinloss Abbey in Moray today.

Robert Corbet

No other references linking Robert Corbet, Lethnot and Troup have been found. Consequently, trying to fix the date of the grant to Kinloss Abbey and identifying further information about Corbet will have to draw on wider considerations. That is the purpose of this section.

Like many families in this period, successive generations had the same first name. The convention used here is that Robert (Corbet) I was the father of Robert (Corbet) II who in turn was the father of Robert (Corbet) III. It should be stressed that these designations are based on the author's interpretation of the, usually very limited, evidence. With that caveat, let us proceed.

A Robert Corbet (Robert II) is known to have been closely associated with David I and is a signatory of charters of the king up to 1136 (Barrow, 1999, 54-60). This Robert's father, Robert I, had accompanied the Norman invasion and received large estates in Shropshire and Northampton. Corbets also settled in Teviotdale which was part of the estates of David I before he came to the throne in 1124 (Black, 1946, 170). Barrow includes Robert II as one of the men 'closely tied' to King David who 'through personal service still attend him in Scotland where their dynastic ambitions would in many cases find ample fulfilment' (Barrow, 1999, 20). Coutts states that the Robert II, the friend of David I, came from Drayton in the county of Northampton (Coutts, 1922, 106).

Robert II was the father of Walter Corbet, later sheriff of Roxburgh and one of the hostages given up by William the Lion to King Henry of England at Falaise in 1174 (Bain, 1881, #139). Walter Corbet was the older son. He married a daughter of Gilbert de Umfraville, a family with well known associations to both Scottish and English events at this period. Walter had a younger brother, Robert III; the seals of a Robert Corbet and Walter Corbet are attached to charters granting land to Melrose Abbey about 1170 (Black, 1946, 170). Marriage into the Umfraville family would have been a step up the political ladder for the Corbets (Beam, 2009, 28-30).

The Corbets are not the only family who may have been allocated land along the north-east coast at this time. One of the witnesses to the Melrose charters was Ralph Le Neym who had a similar background to Robert Corbet and who had also granted land to Melrose Abbey. He was granted lands at St Fergus at about the same time. Bannerman states that Le Neym and Corbet were 'neighbours' both in the south and in the north (Bannerman, 1895, 24). A further similarity is that a Ralf Le Neym made a grant in the early years of the thirteenth century of the church of Inverugie (Barrow, 1980, 188) to the monastery of Arbroath (established in 1178 and a Tironensian foundation). Intriguingly the parish of St Fergus was a detached part of Banffshire prior to boundary reorganization in 1890, suggesting a potential link between Le Neym and people further west. Another family linked to this area was the Barclays (or Berkeleys) who may have been at Cullen (or Colen) near Auldhaven in Glendowachy from the twelfth century (Barclay, 1933, 43).

What can be deduced from this? First, it is not certain how many generations of Corbet cover the time span here; the designation of I, II, or III for 3 generations represents a likely interpretation of known evidence. It is reasonable to associate one generation of Corbets with Troup, and to agree with Bannerman that Robert Corbet must have been in possession of the lands of Troup before he could re-assign a portion of them (Bannerman, 1897, 15). In his view, the lands of Troup must have been a defined entity by the time of the grant to Kinloss. The key question is which Robert Corbet.

The earliest possibility arises from the well-attested link between David I and Robert Corbet. This would mean that an allocation of lands to Robert II was made before 1153, the year of David I's death. Such a date would fit with the only surviving dated charter of David I written at Banff which Barrow places in the period 1145 to 1153. A subsequent allocation by Robert II to Kinloss Abbey would not only show loyalty to a valued royal patron but would also be typical behaviour for an Anglo-Norman nobleman of the period, as demonstrated by the grant to Melrose mentioned above. In confirming that the monks of Kinloss came from Melrose, Bannerman also states that they were Robert Corbet's "ain folk". In this scenario the grant of lands to Kinloss could have been as early as 1150-53. However, it must be remembered that the allocation of lands to Robert II does not necessarily imply an immediate allocation to Kinloss.

The lands of Lethnot are located within the parish of Gamrie. William I (the Lion) was also active in the north-east in the twelfth century. He established the parish of Gamrie between 1189 and 1198, bestowing the church of Gamrie upon his favourite Abbey of Arbroath (Spalding Club, 1843, 489), a grant renewed in the future, for example in 1257 (Reg. Aber., 1885, 22). The grant of land was confirmed by the Bishops of Aberdeen, namely Bishop Matthew (between 1189 and 1199), Bishop John (1199 to 1207), and Bishop Adam (between 1207 and 1228). It is important to note that the grant mentioned the church of Gamrie on More Head (NJ 791645) along with the chapel of Troup, written as 'trub'.

Bannerman argues that, had Gamrie been a parish when Lethnot was granted to Kinloss, the gift would have been subject to the payment of tithes because, as Church property, tithes could not be alienated by the feudal overlord. As there is no record of these tithes in the records of Arbroath Abbey, the Diocese of Aberdeen or Kinloss Abbey, Bannerman's explanation is that the gift of land preceded Gamrie being a parish, or part of a parish. Thus 1198 is the latest date for the grant to Kinloss.

It can be argued that the lengthy window of time (from 1150 to 1198) for the grant to Kinloss can be narrowed. Arbroath Abbey was founded in 1178 and was known to be a favourite of King William. This provides a second possibility; namely, the grant of Lethnot to Kinloss was made by Robert III, perhaps about the same time (1170) as the grant to Melrose mentioned above. The apparent lack of references to Robert II after 1136 may strengthen the case for the grant being by Robert III.

A photo from the Bodie Collection; date unknown. The view is over the remains of St John's Church and the Gamrie graveyard. We see the full sweep of Gamrie Bay to the east with Crovie and Lethnot visible in the distance. This photo was taken before the modern expansion of Gardenstown. We see only the older Gardenstown, tucked in at the foot of the cliff.

In this context it is useful to note the comments from a recent scholar of medieval Scotland. Alice Taylor compares the practice of David I and William the Lion in granting land. William 'predominantly gave smaller gifts of land north of the Forth not only to the descendants of settlers and people who had newly appeared in his kingdom but also to men whose existing familial status placed them among the major players in those areas.' (Taylor, 2016, 439)

It has been argued, plausibly, that at its formation the parish of Gamrie consisted of two feudal territories, Glendowachy, immediately to the west of Troup, and Troup, defining an area along the Banffshire coast from the mouth of the Deveron east to Nethermill (Bannerman, 1897, 14). No reference exists to a thanage at Troup, although the existence of the thanage of Glendowachy is well attested. It was a royal thanage, at least by the later thirteenth century in the reign of Alexander III (Grant, 1993, 61 & 73). After 1365, it is also known as Doune (or Doun), a name still current in the area, but Glendowachy remained in use in some later charters.

It may be that, late in the twelfth century, William I confirmed, consolidated or extended what King David had begun. The match between the eastern and southern boundaries of the parish of Gamrie and the likely boundaries of Troup would support this view.

An engraving showing Arbroath Abbey. As so often, the scale and extent of ecclesiastical building in the medieval period contrasts markedly with that of all others, except royalty.

To summarise, from the perspective of the Scottish crown in the twelfth century, there were compelling reasons for trying to pacify and contain Moray thereby extending the area of stable and loyal local government. Military activity was an important part of this strategy but so too was the creation of a framework of civil and ecclesiastical governance, as outlined above. The area east of the river Spey, generally acknowledged as the eastern boundary of Moray, to the western boundary of Buchan, including Troup, would have been of particular concern in containing Moray.

From the evidence so far identified, it is not possible to be precise about the date of establishment of the lands of Troup as a defined entity. However, the discussion above points to the conclusion that incoming settlement of Troup took place in the latter half of the twelfth century.

Who Lived at Troup?

The probability is that Robert Corbet (II or III) was granted the lands of Troup. Within the Troup area, at least three locations are possible for settlement in the twelfth century. Both Findon (NJ 795643) and Crovie (NJ 810663) have been identified as mottes which, if accepted, would also support likely twelfth century occupation. Neither of these has been excavated or has yielded dating evidence of such occupation. More than one twelfth century settlement within the lands of Troup would not be surprising. However, it would be a surprise if the description in 1868 of The Law of Crovie in the Ordnance Survey Name Book for Banffshire as 'the ancient place of execution of the Thane of Lightnot' proved accurate.

The likeliest known site for a settlement at that time is the house on the Knoll at Cullykhan. Given the nature of some of the finds on the Knoll, and later development of the castle on Cullykhan, it could be argued that this location was the most prestigious one in the immediate area.

Although there are many references to Corbets subsequently, the individuals named are associated with southern Scotland, where the major Corbet landholdings were located, and England. No documentary evidence has been found to indicate what happened to Robert Corbet, or any successors, in north-east Scotland. Ritchie notes that Robert Corbet 'prematurely' disappears from the records (Ritchie, 1954, 216). Apart from death, another possibility to explain Robert Corbet's 'disappearance' is that he returned home leaving colonial effort to younger or more energetic kinsmen.

Unresolved Questions

The first is why Lethnot is defined as it is, and what this may mean for other features in the area at that particular time. Was access to the sea important? Did it border lands already attached to the church of Gamrie? Was its position between two mottes, at Findon and Crovie, significant? Was it a combination of some of these together with clarity of definition of boundaries? Was it already a defined entity? Appendix 1 contains all the relevant information found for informed speculation. One relevant factor may be that the beach at Gamrie provided access for travel by sea, similar to Cullykhan, and the potential travel route south up the Den of Afforsk.

This view is taken from More Head to the west of Gardenstown, looking over the remains of St John's Church with the site of Findon in the centre. The prominence of Findon is clear, as is its identification as a likely motte. This is a site where excavation could resolve that issue, as well as whether it was a place of earlier settlement matching the reported sighting of fragments of vitrification here. To the right the Den of Afforsk runs south. To the left the part of the beach and settlement at Gardenstown are visible.

The second issue is the location of the chapel of Troup. The first point to emphasise relating to the references mentioned above is that it is an early building, from possibly as early as the twelfth century. Some have associated it with the place called Chapelden in the Tore of Troup. There is a useful description of this place in the New Statistical Account. The critical point here is that this site is in the land of Auchmedden in the parish of Aberdour and not in the parish of Gamrie or the lands of Troup. Like many early places of worship it is close to a boundary and to running water but the strong probability is that the site was a place of worship for Auchmedden or Glencuthil within the earldom of Buchan, and not in Troup.

No firm identification, based on archaeological or historical evidence can be made for a chapel site in Troup. One local publication has suggested Northfield as a possible location. Interestingly, there is a direct line of sight from St. John's Kirk on More Head to Northfield. The archaeological evidence does not appear to support the Knoll on Cullykhan as the location.

Into the Thirteenth Century: the Comyns

Apart from the allusions to Lethnot mentioned above, the next reference concerning Troup is late thirteenth century, and is associated with the name Hamelin de Trop. Clearly this name signifies a family taking its name from the land with which it is connected. Also in the same time period, the date of construction of the castle on Cullykhan has to be a significant consideration.

It may be that occupation on Cullykhan was continuous from the construction of the house on the Knoll to the building of the castle but that cannot be concluded with certainty either from archaeological or historical evidence. Historical evidence does point to ongoing activity in the area from early in the thirteenth century with the direct involvement of the Comyns in neighbouring Buchan, all of which is relevant to the story.

At the beginning of the thirteenth century, the male line of the Celtic mormaers or earls of Buchan ended. Marjory, daughter and heiress of Fergus the last earl, married William Comyn, probably in 1210 and certainly by 1212. As was customary at that time, he became earl of Buchan when Fergus died thereby becoming the first 'Norman' earl in Scotland. Since 1205, William had held the important Scottish office of justiciar. William also founded the Abbey of Deer in 1219 with a colony of Cistercians from Kinloss. He died in 1233 and was succeeded as earl by his son Alexander who in turn was succeeded by his son John in 1289.

The Comyn family had major landholdings elsewhere, for example in Badenoch and Kilbride. They had been in the vanguard of Anglo-Norman advancement in Scotland since the reign of David I. In the reign of

Alexander III the Comyns had 3 earls, 1 baron and 30 knights of that name settled in various parts of the country (Spence, 1873, 19). That may or may not be exact but such numbers imply some degree of importance.

Given the closeness of the parties to the royal court it is likely that some Corbets and some Comyns knew each other. Slightly later, in 1248, there is also a reference demonstrating possible links between the Berkeleys, who built Culen castle in Glendowachy to the west of Troup, and the Comyns (Barclay, 1933, 47).

Generally, the Comyns were great acquirers of territory. As one of the most powerful families in Scotland in the thirteenth century, they exercised their influence by strategic marriages (as in Buchan) or by other means (Brown, 2004, 171). For example, they expanded the boundaries of their Buchan lands by including Formartine and Belhelvie (Young, 1993, 197). They viewed Buchan as their key landholding even after they acquired, by inheritance, the substantial de Quincy estates with significant holdings in England.

It is not credible that the Comyns would have tolerated any power vacuum on the western boundary of Buchan. Equally, it is hard to believe that they would look kindly on settlement there by those opposed to their interests. If there was not continuous settlement at Troup, the Comyns would surely have filled the gap quickly. The presence of the Comyns as neighbours supports the view that occupation of Troup would have been continuous.

Who Were the de Trops?

Three possible origins of the de Trops seem worthy of consideration. The first is that the de Trops were established at Troup by the Corbets; indeed they may be direct descendants. The second, which is not necessarily inconsistent with the first, is that the de Trops were introduced by the Comyns, and had a prior connection with them. The third possibility is that the family which lived on Cullykhan was the 'native' family prior to the arrival of the Comyns and the Corbetts.

This third option is the least likely. Although Gaelic relations of the last mormaer of Buchan are mentioned in the record, and such references continue even after the Comyn marriage and subsequent inheritance of the earldom of Buchan, no record relating to land west of Buchan has been found. The arguments advanced above in relation to the granting of Lethnot to Robert Corbet, the involvement of William I in the area, and the likelihood of what this meant for Troup are persuasive in suggesting that the lands of Troup were under the control of families of Anglo-Norman descent from at least the mid twelfth century onwards. Hamelin is not a Gaelic name.

The other two options have overlapping elements. The Corbets and the Comyns probably were well known to each other and, even if not close allies, had a shared perspective of service and loyalty to the Scottish crown. They would have been acutely conscious of the power and influence of their neighbours to the east and south.

One previously published statement about the origins of the de Trops can be refuted. It has been claimed that 'William Comyn, the first Norman earl of Buchan, settled his vassal Simon de Trop in the castle of Cullykhan'. One reference has been found to a Simon de Trop (Bain, 1881, 283). The content of the reference has no relevance to the north east of Scotland or the Comyns; the date, 1241, is a significant mismatch with the dates of William Comyn who died in 1233. The possible link may be to Trolhop or Trowup in the College Valley in Northumberland. In short, no evidence has been found linking a Simon de Trop to Troup in Banffshire.

There is nothing in the historical record to confirm whether the de Trops were Comyn allies; subsequent events could be used to support both a positive and negative argument on this point. On balance, given the clear and sustained definition of the lands of Buchan to the east and the early reference to Robert Corbet, it may be that the de Trops were closely linked to the Corbets. However, each family is likely to have been well known to the others. Given, too, that this area, Buchan plus the lands immediately to the west of it, is generally seen as an area governed by loyal followers of the king, all those concerned may have been aligned with the same faction.

No charter approving the construction of the castle on Cullykhan has been found. Thus determining who built it and when has to draw on wider evidence. One consideration which may be relevant arises from the proximity of the Comyns and their activities. Young states that the period after 1260 saw a burst of building activity by the Buchan Comyns, comparable to corresponding activity by the Badenoch Comyns. In addition to two almshouses (1261 and 1272), an extensive castle building programme in Buchan took place at Slains, Kingedward (immediately to the south of Troup, and in existence by 1273), Cairnbulg and Rattray (Young, 1997, 150). If the neighbours, whether or not they are allies, are taking such steps then it is not unreasonable to imagine similar activity at Troup. The royal castle at Banff was in existence by 1290. The excavations on Cullykhan produced finds, both in the ditch to the west of the Knoll and on the castle site, which provides evidence of activity on the site in the thirteenth century.

A reasonable conclusion from the above is that the initial phase of construction of the castle on Cullykhan was undertaken by the de Trop family in the latter part of the thirteenth century.

At the end of that century, Scotland entered a prolonged period of disruption, violence and war. Troup entered a period where there is more information about the people who lived there and the political context in which they found themselves.

6. THE de TROPS

Setting the Scene

The first named de Trop in the record in Scotland is Hamelin. While his origins may be uncertain, there is no doubt at least two Hamelins existed. Given the number and nature of the references below, it is more appropriate to ask how many Hamelins there were. As will be seen, some of the references are specific in terms of events and people and, where appropriate, the approach taken here is to contextualize these references, for example by mentioning local or national developments, while trying to maintain the narrative. However, gaps in the record mean that the answers to some important questions are not clear.

Before turning to the clearest references, a reference, which may be the earliest one, should be considered. On 28 August 1296 at Berwick on Tweed "Hamund de Trop" is included on the Ragman Roll, a list commissioned by Edward I of all landholders in Scotland, (Bain, 1884, 198). However, in an appendix, Bain lists the seals attached at the ceremony. Here the seal is described as "Hamelin de Trup" (Bain, 1884, 550). It is reasonable to consider Hamund as a transcription error; many names were transcribed that day. There is no other reference to Troup in the Ragman Roll. The document indicates that Hamund/Hamelin came from Lanarkshire. Research in Lanarkshire has found no reference to a Hamund/Hamelin or Troup there.

The Ragman Roll was collated at numerous venues around Scotland, including Banff and Aberdeen where local names, on 17 July 1296, included Duncan de Ferndraught and Reginald le Chen, both of whom will feature in the story soon. However, Barrow is of the view that the seals were gathered by sheriffs and forwarded to the parliament at Berwick; not all those who were recorded at Berwick would have attended (Barrow, 1976, 107). Many locations were represented; there was potential for confusion about names and their landholdings, especially if the record was compiled by clerks unfamiliar with Scotland.

On balance, it is likely that this signature represents the first link between a named individual, Hamelin, and the lands of Troup.

A summary list of all the Hamelin references may assist in following the narrative.

1296 Hamund de Trop on Ragman Roll (see above).
1304 Hamelin does homage to Edward I at St Andrews.
1304 First petition to Edward I by Hamelin de Trop (son).
1305 Two further petitions to Edward I by Hamelin de Trop,
      one jointly by father and son.
1306 Hamelin de Trop with Robert Bruce.
      Hamelin in a list of Scottish landowners forfeited.
1320 de Soules conspiracy; Hamelin accused but acquitted.
1328 Hamelin de Trupp is sheriff of Banff.
1332 Papal letter granting prebend to Hamelin de Troup.
1335 Hamelin de Troup dies.
1337 English King grants pension to Elyne, widow of Hamelin de Troup.
1342 Grant of Troup to Andrew Buttergask.
1345 Pope grants petition to Hamelin de Trup for church of Inchbrioc.

The second reference indicates that Hamelin de Trop, with many others, did homage to Edward I at the parliament at St Andrews in March 1304 (Palgrave, 1837, 299). Another person recorded was Phy de Fyndon though it is more likely, taking account of the actual record and the terms of the petition below, that this is a reference to Kincardine rather than Findon in Troup. Findon is one of a number of place names in Troup which occur in other parts of Scotland.

The de Trop Petitions

There are three petitions in 1304/5 to Edward I in the Rolls of (the English) Parliament from Hamelin de Trop, father or son or both, which illuminate vividly the state of Scotland at that time. Two people named in these petitions are Sir Reginald le Chen and Duncan de Frendraught. Some background on them is useful.

Both le Chen and Frendraught held positions in Edward I's administration of the north of Scotland. Frendraught, whose lands were on the Banffshire/Aberdeenshire border in the parish of Forgue, was a lieutenant north of the Forth, keeper of the King's forest of Enzie, and sheriff of Banff. The length of time these posts were held is not always easy to ascertain. However, the first two of these can be dated to 1304;

the dating of the third appears to overlap the timing of the petitions. Frendraught was still well known as a Comyn ally in 1307 (Young, 1993, 203). He may well have fought and died on the English side at Bannockburn in 1314, as his widow Marjory received a grant of 43 pounds from Edward II 'for her sustenance'.

The Le Chen castles at Duffus and Ravenscraig in Moray were attacked and burnt in the wars of 1297 and 1304. Reginald is known as a strong and consistent supporter of Edward I and the Comyns. He was made justiciar north of the Mounth by Edward I in September 1305 along with John de Vaux of Northumberland. In short the loyalties of both these men are clear over the period in question here.

Duffus Castle is in Moray. The first construction was a motte (still clearly visible) and bailey. Originally it was surrounded by the waters of the Loch of Spynie, now drained to form part of the fertile Laich of Moray between Elgin and the coast.

In the first petition, Hamelin the son states that Reginald le Chen came by night, with his own force and that of Duncan de Frendraught, to Hamelin's lands of Findon and Logie, trampled his corn and consumed it, preventing him from having profit from his land, "as the good people of Scotland can attest". He stated that it would be impossible for him to retain possession of his lands on account of these knights, "unless the King put a stop to their proceedings". He requests a remedy.

In response to this, Edward orders that the petitioner should have a writ to his lieutenant in Scotland to call parties before him, and having inquired into the truth of the statements in the petition, to do justice in the case. It appears that some action was taken, although given the status of le Chen and Frendraught the identity of the person who dealt with the petition would be useful to know.

The Seatown of modern Gardenstown clings to the shore. Behind, in the centre right, is the conical site called Findon, mentioned in the de Trop petitions. Further to its right heading inland is the Den of Afforsk, which is a possible route for the raiders coming from the south. This picture was taken from the eastern end of Crovie.

In the second petition, Hamelin de Trop, the father, and Hamelin, the son, petitioned the King and Council for redress for the injuries done to them by Sir Duncan de Frendraught, Sheriff of Banff, who had sent his people at the dead of night to the lands of Findon, belonging to Hamelin, the son, and burned his houses and took and imprisoned his people against the peace. (Although there are similarities with the first petition, the detail suggests that this represents further raiding.) They complained that he had disobeyed the orders which the Guardian gave on their last petition, inasmuch as he had only delivered up a half of the property belonging to Hamelin, the father, and had not observed that officer's injunction not to molest or injure the Hamelins, but had assembled the

63

force of his bailiwick, and, after pillaging the land, had taken and imprisoned their people and held them contrary to the pledge. They also alleged that Frendraught made himself judge in all manner of pleas concerning the Hamelins, although he was a party and their adversary.

The raids are described as being in lands towards the south and west of Troup (see Appendix 1). Given the known bases of Frendraught, in particular, and le Chen, that is perhaps to be expected, although the proximity to Kingedward, a known Comyn stronghold, may be just as significant; it could have served as a convenient 'jumping off' point for action. Even today, it is not difficult to imagine how intimidating it would be to experience an attack, perhaps on horseback, of powerful men sweeping down through the lands of Logie towards Findon and the coast.

Edward's response to this petition was the same as to the first one.

In the third petition, Hamelin de Trop complained that Sir Duncan de Frendraught resided in the Regality of the Abbey of Arbroath and maintained thieves and robbers there, and that the thieves had robbed Thomas le Graunt of all his goods and chattels and cut off one of his hands. After the attack the marauders repaired to Sir Duncan's residence where they were protected by him within the Liberties of the Abbey, contrary to the peace of the King. It is further stated that no one would live with his people in his Franchise on account of Sir Duncan (Taylor, 1858, 271). Taylor believes that the regality referred to was Aberchirder, the church of which, with a davoch of land annexed to it, had been given by Bricius, Bishop of Moray, to the Abbey of Arbroath early in the thirteenth century (Bannatyne Club, 1837, 251-2).

Again Edward's response was the same.

Before considering what these petitions may tell us, two other events seem particularly relevant. First, in late September 1305 Sir Walter Barclay was appointed sheriff of Banff by Edward I in the same list of appointments as Reginald le Chen, all of which were designed to produce, from Edward's perspective, a settled governance of Scotland at that time. The second event is that in 1306, only months after the last petition (which may be dated to October 1305), Hamelin had joined Robert Bruce (Barrow, 1976, 158). Bruce had killed John Comyn of Badenoch, a cousin of the John Comyn who was earl of Buchan, in Dumfries on 10 February 1306, and was enthroned at Scone in March.

Looking at the three petitions, although there may be some repetition, the texts suggest an escalation in violence and potential lawlessness from the first to the third. While it is reasonable to consider that the first petition set in process the sequence of events which followed, it is possible that the actions described in it were prompted by earlier events, not in the record.

Another possibility is that there was an earlier incursion, or grievance, arising from actions of one of the Hamelins. The Troup lands at Logie are near the likely boundary with Kingedward, part of the earldom of Buchan; the proximity of a border can provide the potential for disputes.

A final point is that the allegation in the second petition that Duncan de Frendraught had been unfair to the de Trops in his dealings as sheriff of Banff may predate the first raid. The statement in the second petition that Frendraught "had only delivered up half the property belonging to Hamelin the father" may indicate this. In other words the events described in the petitions may be the culmination of earlier disputes.

Loyalties of Hamelin

There is no indication of Hamelin's loyalties during the campaign of Andrew Murray into the north-east in 1297. Equally, it is not known whether there was any contact with Edward I when he was in the area in 1303. Possibly of significance in this context is Taylor's description of Edward's passage on a coastal route through Buchan in 1303. Taylor speculates that Edward may have stopped off at Dundarg Castle and at a de Trop castle (Taylor, 1858, 210). Any direct contact with King Edward, either locally or at the St Andrews parliament, may have encouraged Hamelin to have a positive view of King Edward and believe that he would receive a fair hearing and favourable outcome to his grievances. Having done homage, Hamelin would naturally expect justice from his overlord.

At the same time it was clear that Edward I was the real power in Scotland at this time and, as such, was the ultimate arbiter and administrator of justice. If the de Trops wished to pursue their claims, it would have to be via Edward.

This was a period when loyalties undoubtedly could and did change - sometimes more than once - for any number of reasons. However, it is hard to conceive that the raids described above could have been carried out so close to the Comyn stronghold of Buchan, by known allies of the

Comyns, if the de Trops were also firm allies, or under the protection, of the Comyns. Conversely, Hamelin's loyalties may have been viewed with suspicion by those whom he accused. They may have acted with or without the connivance of the Comyns. For example, the Comyns may have wanted to enlarge their landholding. Pragmatically, they may have been trying to improve the security of Buchan in the direction of Moray, as Robert the Bruce and his followers were campaigning in that area.

Returning to the petitions; the de Trops acknowledge that some action was taken as a result of the first petition. Perhaps it is significant that le Chen was named only in the first one. Was his absence from the others an indication of action taken or that he had been cleared of any involvement in the initial raid? The second petition could imply the latter as well as indicating further forays by Frendraught. The appointment of Walter Barclay as sheriff of Banff ousted Frendraught from that post. The continuing incursions, and the escalating violence, may be attributed to Frendraught's anger at his loss of status, as well as being fuelled by any personal animosity between him and the de Trops.

Finally the question arises of whether it was a result of these raids that a settlement at Findon was abandoned, and settlement consolidated on a better defended site at Cullykhan with a stone-built castle.

From the perspective of the de Trops, if they were or saw themselves as Comyn adherents or under the protection of the Comyns, these raids would have been a major shock and disruption, whatever the reason for them. It would be difficult to rationalize them as 'a sign of the times'. The absence of an acceptable response to the petitions from those in government, together with a growing appreciation of the predicament in which they found themselves, could certainly have prompted the decision by Hamelin to join Bruce. Professor Barrow includes Hamelin in a group who had presented petitions at the September 1305 Parliament and then were out with Bruce a few months later with a possible common factor being that, they had lost, or felt that they were under the threat of losing, their lands.

Ultimately it is not possible to determine whether Hamelin sided with Bruce because his lands were attacked or whether his lands were raided because he was suspected of, or was, a Bruce sympathizer or supporter. One of the intriguing questions is "Which Hamelin joined Bruce?" The risks associated with such a decision would have been obvious to them, arguing perhaps for one joining Bruce and the other staying to guard the home area. However, perhaps Hamelin should be given credit for shrewdness; there is no evidence, documentary or archaeological, of any attacks on the de Trop stronghold of Cullykhan either before or during the herschip of Buchan in 1308.

A final thought associated with the tangled question of loyalties is worth considering. Walter Barclay was one of the three sheriffs in Scotland (out of seventeen) who joined Bruce after 1306 (Young, 1997, 200). Conceivably, he and Hamelin de Trop were not only neighbours but allies; perhaps support for the Bruce cause had been latent for some time.

Hamelin de Trop and Robert I

When Hamelin joined forces with Bruce in 1306 he was setting himself firmly against his closest and most powerful neighbours. As confirmation of his change of allegiance, Hamelin's name appears in the list of Scottish landowners forfeited by Edward I in 1306 for supporting Robert Bruce (Barrow, 1976, 328); William de Hustveit petitioned to have Hamelin's lands but there is no record that this was successful (Palgrave, 1837, 315).

In the next period, references to Hamelin cease. However events in north-east Scotland moved on apace. The decisive event in Bruce's campaign against the Comyns was the battle of Inverurie or Barra Hill (probably May 1308) at which the earl of Buchan, John Comyn, and his allies were soundly defeated (Young, 1993, 174). The intensity of the enmity was demonstrated by the herschip or harrying of Buchan which followed. Bruce saw the destruction of Buchan as a power centre of the Comyns as essential to the establishment of his kingship. The death of John Comyn later in 1308 helped (Young, 1997, 205) but the physical destruction of men, buildings (including Dundarg Castle), livestock and crops followed by the division of Buchan into a series of baronies under the control of Bruce loyalists ensured a permanent change to the pattern of landholding and government in the north-east.

There is no evidence that Hamelin actually participated in these events or benefited materially from a presumed participation with Bruce's supporters. Although the Comyns' power was broken and their lands forfeited, many lesser landowners kept their lands in Buchan (Young, 1993, 199). There is no mention of Troup at this time in the records.

One interpretation of the events is that the raids by Frendraught and/or le Chen meant a de facto diminution of land for the de Trops. With the Bruce victory in the north-east, all these lands were firmly established under the de Trops with Glendowachy also confirmed to the Berkeleys. This may have constituted the recognition by Robert the Bruce for support given. However, as someone who may have perceived himself as taking a great risk in siding with Bruce, Hamelin may have felt that this was not an over-generous reward for his actions. The possibility - which, given subsequent events, may be more likely - that the de Trops were not perceived as people who displayed lasting loyalties, to either faction, should not be discounted when weighing up any 'rewards'.

The de Soules Conspiracy

There is a time gap in the references. When the name Hamelin reappears in the record, the question of loyalties surfaces again.

The Grenago Stane

There are many legends associated with Robert Bruce, and indeed William Wallace. One of these concerns the battle of Inverurie or Barra Hill in May 1308 where Bruce's forces defeated the combined supporters of the Comyns in Buchan. This was a key event in the history of Buchan as it led to the dismemberment of the great earldom of Buchan.

Behind the Grenago Stane (or 'Groaning Stone') supposedly is where the vanquished Earl of Buchan lay, groaning and moaning about the loss of his forces, the battle and his future. The stone – almost certainly part of a former stone circle – is now a feature, or should that be a hazard, on the 14th fairway of Oldmeldrum golf course.

In 1320, a Hamelin de Troup, described as an esquire, was accused of being part of the de Soules conspiracy. King Robert I saw the conspiracy as a serious plot against him and the Bruce succession (Penman, 1999, 25). This was reflected in the punishments given, including execution, to those whose guilt was established to the king's satisfaction.

Although Hamelin was acquitted in the de Soules conspiracy, some of the factors said to have contributed to the development of the conspiracy may be relevant to his position. Two in particular are worth highlighting. First, undoubtedly, it was seen as an attempted coup by, the Balliol faction. Countess Agnes of Strathearn, widow of Malise sixth earl of Strathearn and a daughter of Alexander Comyn late earl of Buchan, was deemed to be one of the ringleaders. Penman, in his detailed account of the conspiracy and its motivation includes Hamelin, along with Eustace Maxwell, Walter Barclay (who also had joined Bruce in 1306), Patrick Graham and Eustace Rattray, in a group who either had a record of support for Balliol/Comyn patriots and/or service to the English Crown (Edward I, II, III). The second factor which Penman highlights is a sense of grievance about the approach used and decisions made by King Robert in allocating forfeited lands in the years following Bannockburn; a significant number of the conspirators felt that they had valid claims which the king had not recognised. Did Hamelin continue to harbour grievances about the settlement of lands in the wider Buchan area as Bruce introduced families from elsewhere, in whom perhaps he had greater trust, in his allocation of the substantial Comyn lands?

Perhaps all that we can draw from the limited source material specifically referring to Hamelin, is that Hamelin was associated to some degree with people whose sympathies were pro-Balliol and anti-Bruce, some of whom felt they had been ill done by in terms of their rights to land.

Nevertheless, at some point after the conspiracy, Hamelin's loyalty was deemed sufficiently secure to make him sheriff of Banff. This happened at an unknown date before 1328 when Hamelin as sheriff receives a 'contribution for peace for the term of Whitsunday' (Stuart and Burnett Vol. I, 1878, 106). No date is known for when Hamelin ceased to be sheriff. Penman has suggested that appointments such as this may be an attempt to secure the loyalty of the individuals concerned.

The theme of loyalties will be revisited, later in this chapter.

Final References to Hamelin de Trop

There are five further references to a Hamelin de Trop covering the period 1332 to 1345. Two of these, dated 1332 and 1345 respectively, appear to be linked. The first is a letter from the Pope in Avignon, with a concurrent mandate to the bishop of Aberdeen and the Abbot of Deer, for the provision of a canonry and prebend of Aberdeen to Hamelin de Troup (Bliss, 1893, #385). A prebend is a share of the revenues of a cathedral or collegiate church allowed to a clergyman who officiates at stated times. At this time the only prebend churches in Aberdeen were St Machar, which had a dean, and St Nicholas which was the seat of the bishop (Cowan, 1967, 213).

The reference dated 1345 states that, probably the same Hamelin's petition for the church of Inchbrioc, just south of Montrose (Wilson, 1868, 103), in the diocese of St Andrews was granted, again by the Pope. In the record, Hamelin is described as an advanced scholar and bachelor of law of the diocese of Aberdeen. It is stated that he was ready to resign his current church at Logry, in the diocese of Aberdeen, to move to Inchbrioc which was void due to the neglect of John de Lambertoun (Bliss, 1893, 86). The church at Inchbriock, in the diocese of St Andrews, was dedicated to St Braoch in 1243. It was granted again in 1351 to John de Litton, perhaps indicating the death of Hamelin. The original site of the church can still be visited, although the church was a ruin by 1573.

Two further references, dated 1335 and 1337/8, are also linked. In the first, it is stated that Hamelin de Troup died "in the service of Edward III shortly before February 1335". The second reference reads that 'for the great compassion he (i.e. King Edward III of England) has for the condition of Elyne the widow of Hamelyne de Troupe who lately died in his service in Scotland, grants her to keep herself and her children 6s. 8d. a week' (Bain, 1887, 230).

Before further considering the context and implications of this evidence, the final reference, dated 1342, merits attention. 'Sometime that year (1342), the aforementioned royal servant Andrew Buttergask received extensive lands and forestry in Banffshire, including the baronies of Westford and Troup, the latter forfeited by Hamelin of Troup, sheriff of Banff and an Edward Balliol supporter acquitted of a part in the conspiracy of 1320' (Penman, 2004, 95).

70

Hamelin and the Balliols

These statements show a clear alignment between Hamelin and Edward Balliol and indeed Edward III. The possible Balliol sympathies of 1320 appear to have flourished in the 1330s, after an interregnum as a Bruce-appointed sheriff. As in 1320, the legacy and distribution of the Comyn lands in Buchan, particularly those adjoining Troup, may be the root cause of Hamelin's views.

The Disinherited were a group of predominantly English knights and lords who had lost their lands in Scotland as a direct result of action taken by Robert I who redistributed their lands to those who had supported him. They were a powerful and influential group who felt their disaffection keenly and who tried to persuade Edward III, as their feudal overlord and monarch, to take action in Scotland to restore their lands. In truth, this served at times as a very useful pretext for Edward to lead or authorize forces to invade Scotland repeatedly in the 1330s.

One of the key leaders of the Disinherited was Henry Beaumont who claimed the earldom of Buchan through his wife, Alice Comyn, a daughter of the last Comyn earl of Buchan. She and Beaumont believed that her share of the lands of Buchan included the estate of Aberdour bordering Troup to the east and including Dundarg Castle.

Henry Beaumont was a key leader of an army from England which invaded Scotland and initially made good progress. The invaders won the battle of Dupplin Moor in 1332, established the position of Edward Balliol as King of Scotland and restored some land to the Disinherited. In particular, Dundarg castle was rebuilt, probably in haste, in 1333 and occupied by English forces led by Beaumont. Perhaps at this point Hamelin committed himself to the Balliol/English faction. The success of this faction on his doorstep may have created the impression that they were going to be 'the winning side', with the possibility of reward.

However, spring and summer 1334 saw a steady improvement for the Bruce party. By the winter of 1334 Beaumont and his followers were under siege in Dundarg Castle without any early prospect of relief by Edward III. Beaumont, with 'failing provisions and despairing of relief' (Rogers, 2000, 86), surrendered on 23 December on terms, including a safe conduct to England for his household, and the castle fell (Watt, 1996,

95 & 119). If the February 1335 date is correct, then the likelihood, given the terms of the award of the pension to his widow, is that Hamelin was killed or fatally injured at this point.

This aerial view of the promontory on which Dundarg Castle sits shows the similarities with the site at Cullykhan. On the landward side, ditches added further defences.

Two other possibilities are worthy of consideration. First, Hamelin may have been a casualty in 1335 at Culblean in Mar where David Strathbogie, a key Balliol supporter, was defeated and killed in a battle with Bruce forces led by Andrew Murray. The second possibility could be linked to Edward III campaigning in the north of Scotland in 1336. Initially, he raised the siege of Lochindorb Castle, where the Countess of Atholl, who was Henry Beaumont's daughter, was trapped. In the months that followed, he burned Forres and Aberdeen and laid waste to virtually the entire coast between the Moray Firth and the Tay (Rogers, 2000, 118).

Whatever the motivation of individuals, the outcome for the de Trops was clear. David II followed the pattern of his father in dealing with disloyalty, and disinherited Hamelin de Trop passing the estate, in due course, to Andrew Buttergask.

Discussion of the de Trops

As usual, the paucity of records for this period and place leaves ample scope for conjecture to explain the events described above and fill the gaps in the narrative. This section will focus on two issues primarily – the generations of the de Trops, and the loyalties/affiliations of these generations.

There are references to Hamelins, father and son, in the same text confirming at least two generations. Additionally, it is plausible to believe that the Hamelin who became the churchman is neither of these, and thus we have at least three generations. This Hamelin III is likely to have been in his mid-twenties in 1332, thus making his father, Hamelin II, a mature man by 1306, say. Going back a further generation would make Hamelin I a mature man about 1280, perhaps indicating a date of birth about 1260. If so, Hamelin I would have to be unusually long-lived for the period to be active in Edward III's service until 1335. More likely then, the Hamelin who died in 1335 is Hamelin II.

One approach to the question of loyalties is to consider whether changing loyalties may reflect different generations. Accordingly, episodes which seem at variance with an established pattern of behaviour may be explained most readily by concluding that it is different individuals who are involved.

Support for the Balliol cause seems assured in the events in 1334/5 and may also be attributed, albeit less securely, to the actions associated with the de Soules conspiracy. Less assuredly, because of lack of certainty on the relevant facts, could be affiliation to the Comyns, which would predate all the de Trop references quoted here.

On this analysis the event which stands out as "out of character" is the decision to side with Bruce in 1306. The provocations endured and the injustice felt do provide ample justification particularly if the impetus for the raids arose from a personal grievance between Frendraught and Hamelin I. It makes sense, too, that it would be Hamelin I who forfeited the estate in 1306. It may be that Hamelin I died in Bruce's service. Subsequent references fit more easily with Hamelin II, the esquire in 1320, his loyalty being secured as appointment as sheriff, and the support for Balliol in the 1330s. Perhaps, as indicated above, Hamelin III died about 1350.

In summary, the de Trops' loyalties may have been primarily with the Comyn/Balliol faction, thereby strengthening the case that the Comyns may have been party to their introduction to the area. Under considerable provocation, Hamelin I changed allegiance in 1306. Hamelin II, who may have inherited not long after this date, maintained the traditional family line through to his death around 1335, despite the possible attempt to win him over by his appointment as sheriff of Banff. On this analysis, it is most likely that Hamelin I would have been responsible for building the castle on Cullykhan, perhaps using masons who had been working on Comyn projects.

7. FROM THE de TROPS TO THE KEITHS

The Buttergasks

The name Buttergask and the lands of Troup were linked in 1342. A number of family members feature in the records of the reign of David II, but Andrew Buttergask is the key player for the story of Troup. The family name also appears as Buttercase. It is mostly associated with Perthshire. Indeed, there is still a road sign indicating Buttergask on the A9 south of Perth.

Andrew's brother, Adam, was a member of David II's immediate household and was with King David in France from 1334 to 1341 as clerk to the wardrobe. He acted on occasion as an envoy from David's court in Chateau Gaillard to Scotland. Also present in France was Robert Keith whose family will soon enter the story. Another Buttergask, William, was also a member of the royal household (Stuart & Burnett, 1878, 375).

Chateau Gaillard in Normandy

Andrew, too, was a royal official, but he remained in Scotland. He was depute justiciar north of the Forth in 1334-5 when he asserted that he could not collect the few burgh customs of Aberdeen accessible to the Bruce party and assigned to the exiled royal household because of a dispute between the Steward, who was Lieutenant, and the earl of Moray. By 1337, Andrew was deputy Chamberlain and in 1339, as depute justiciar, he held justice ayres in Elgin and Aberdeen (Penman, 2004, 53, 58-9).

After King David's return, Andrew Buttergask received, in 1342, extensive lands in Banffshire, including the barony of Troup; this may be the first mention of Troup as a barony. He received lands elsewhere in Scotland and, by June 1344 (and probably earlier), was sheriff of Perth (Penman, 2004, 100); he received further lands in Perthshire, Banffshire, Aberdeenshire, Angus and Galloway (Thomson, 1984, 291 & 595).

Given his widely scattered holdings, it is doubtful whether Andrew Buttergask ever lived at Cullykhan even for short periods; the main family lands were in Perthshire. If so, would the castle on Cullykhan otherwise be unoccupied, and perhaps have fallen into some disrepair? Would Elyne de Trop, and family, have remained there?

It is worth quoting Penman in relation to the general conditions in Scotland at this time.

Scotland in 1341, too, can only have given the appearance of a sorely wasted kingdom. Most of the realm's castles and burghs had been razed or burned at least once during the previous decade. The land was scarred and, in many places, barren and unworked after four decades of conflict with only a few years respite after 1323 and between 1328 and 1332; harsh winters had also taken their toll during a European-wide climatic cooling (Penman, 2004, 77).

King David II

Andrew Buttergask was killed, along with many others, at the disastrous Scottish defeat at the battle of Neville's Cross near Durham in 1346 (Penman, 2004, 136). King David was captured and held in England until 1357, a period of time characterised by many modern commentators as an interlude of a rapid and almost total collapse in Scottish royal government and law and order. Crown administrative records for these years have almost completely perished (if they ever existed).

In 1349, during the King's detention in England, Scotland experienced its first major outbreak of plague. Almost a third of Scotland's population perished (Macquarrie, 2004, 191). Some historians now put the death rate higher.

Some chroniclers viewed this disaster as a terrifying punishment merited by the universal sinfulness of men and the violence and greed of magnates, which they record dominated Scotland after Neville's Cross. For many inhabitants of Scotland, this must have been a very difficult, dangerous period; survival would have been a significant challenge.

Exit the de Trops; Enter the Keiths

A number of sources confirm that the line of the de Trops ended with an heiress who married a Keith of the marischal's family. One implication of the marriage is that the lands of Troup were restored to the de Trops, probably sometime after 1346. There is no record of this having happened, though that is not surprising given the conditions in Scotland at that time. However, some pointers to the individuals involved do exist.

One Keith family source (NAS, GD 36/308) states that the heiress was called Matilda and that she was the daughter of Sir Walter Troup of that Ilk. Further relevant information is found in a charter of 1357 in which William Troup, son and heir of John of Troup, gives the lands of Cragy in Kincardine, in the same parish as Inchbrioc, to John Gray of Broxmouth (Spalding Club, 1852, 247).

References to the family of Hamelin and his wife Elyne are few. It seems that Hamelin de Troup II and Elyne had at least two children, Hamelin III and John, who may have had Troup restored to him sometime after 1346. Realistically, he may have been in occupation from 1335 through the Buttergask years to, at least, 1357. If the William in the 1357 charter is the son and heir of John, then Matilda may have been William's (as opposed to Walter's) daughter, or Walter may be a brother of William or of John who succeeded. Simply put, the family ties of the Troup heiress who became Robert Keith's wife remain uncertain.

In keeping with this uncertainty, more than one name has been recorded for the Keith who married the heiress. The most authoritative sources agree that it was Sir Robert Keith, son of Sir William Keith, marischal of Scotland, who became the first Keith of Troup (Innes, 1927, 280; Douglas, 1813, 188). Robert was the second son of Sir William and his wife Margaret Fraser, heiress of John Fraser of Cowie and his wife Mary, who was a sister of Robert I. Robert had two brothers and four or five sisters. Sir William was marischal of Scotland from 1354; he died around 1408, and certainly before the end of 1410.

Robert had an elder brother John who married Jean, a daughter of Robert II. John was identified as his father's heir in a charter of 1373/4. However John died sometime before 27 December 1375 leaving a son, also Robert, who in turn had died by August 1404, or probably slightly earlier. In short, Robert, husband of the heiress of Troup and the first Keith of Troup, became the heir who succeeded as marischal on the death of his father.

No dated contract has been found for Robert's marriage. Nevertheless, Douglas asserts that it took place 'in his elder brother's lifetime' i.e. before the end of 1375 (Douglas, 1813, 188). In that year also, Sir William set out for Robert, in a charter, various lands in Kincardine (parts of the thanage of Cowie and Strachan). These had come into the Keith family from Sir William's marriage. That would support the view that Robert's marriage took place about then.

The first surviving written evidence linking Robert Keith to Troup is a charter of March 1406 in which Robert, duke of Albany, governor of Scotland, confirmed two charters by Sir William Keith to Robert (Thomson, 1984, #883, 884). The terms of this charter make it clear that Robert Keith was already lord of Troup. The implication is that an earlier charter, now lost, must have existed which formally assigned the lands to him. Unfortunately an exact date when Robert Keith assumed the inheritance of Troup is not known.

The documentary evidence does not resolve the question of whether the castle on Cullykhan was occupied continuously. However, a date in the late decades of the fourteenth century for the Keith acquisition of Troup could be consistent with the archaeological evidence from the excavations on the Castle Site. As described there (Greig M, 2013, 312), the phase two and/or phase three outbuildings, rooms 3, 4 and 5, to the south-east of the original tower may date from this period; see Castle Site Plan on p22. Certainly it is reasonable to expect some work on the castle to coincide with the establishment of the Keiths of Troup.

Background of the Keiths

The immediate family background of Robert Keith of Troup was given above. As indicated, the Keiths were a significant family in both a Scottish and north-east context. The surname Keith originated in East Lothian, derived from lands of that name. The move to the north-east of Scotland arose from the break-up of the Comyn earldom of Buchan in the early fourteenth century. Sir Robert de Keith, the then marischal, received Aden in 1309; his brother Edward was also granted former Comyn lands, including Ellon and Methlick. This Sir Robert had command of the Scottish cavalry at the battle of Bannockburn and, in recognition of his service for his King and country, the position of marischal was confirmed as hereditary at the Parliament in Perth in 1320 (Paul, 1909, 31). The role of the marischal was to protect the king's person when attending parliament, and to be custodian of the Royal Regalia of Scotland.

The main line of the Keiths descended through the title and lands of the marischal. This line gained enhanced status twice. The first occasion in 1430 was the granting of the title Lord Keith by James I; the second in 1458 was the elevation to the peerage by James II and the title earl Marischal. Understandably, most of the writing about the Keith family follows the events, careers and succession of the principal family line.

From this time, the home and principal estates of the marischal were in the north-east. Like the Comyns, the Keiths were adept at acquiring lands and influence by service, marriage or other means. Three points need to be emphasized. The first is that there were many branches of the Keith family, of which Keith of Troup was only one. It has to be said that the sources consulted on the Keiths are not always consistent, undoubtedly complicated by shared first names in the extended family and, at times, the degree of intermarriage.

The second point is that the Marischal branch of the Keith family was for a lengthy period well connected to the Scottish royal court, and other major families in north-east Scotland. The Marischal, as a hereditary postholder in the royal household, would have been a participant in many of the events of state. As head of a large family, a key ongoing priority for him would be to ensure, and where possible enlarge, the family inheritance in terms of land and influence.

Finally, what follows will concentrate on Troup, although other branches of the family, especially Keith of Northfield, are included as necessary. For a time, perhaps as a result of Robert Keith being the second son and Keith of Troup prior to becoming marischal, it seems that the Troup inheritance was reserved for the second son of the marischal. How long that remained the case is not completely clear.

The Wider Area and Associated Families

By the late fourteenth century, the landholdings and people in the north-east of Scotland had changed significantly from the time of the Comyn earls of Buchan; in particular, the great earldom of Buchan had been subdivided among a number of families. Although this state of affairs could be interpreted as proof that the policy of Robert I towards the north-east had been effective, the situation was not particularly stable. Royal control tended to be weak and there were many, often violent, quarrels over inheritance and land. Before looking in more detail at the Keiths of Troup, it may be useful to describe these changes in the areas around Troup and to illustrate something of the extent of Keith influence. What follows is a brief snapshot of some events near Troup in the years around 1400.

In 1385 the lands and mill of Melrose, which border Troup immediately to the west, were granted by Andrew Barclay (of Gartly) to his sister Janet who was the widow of Sir John of Monymusk (Barclay, 1933, 210). To the west of Melrose the Barclays of Towie still held Cullen. The Barclays and Keiths were linked by marriage (Barclay, 1933, 153) in an earlier generation, as well as through shared duties in Kincardineshire. Both were closely allied with the royal house and court.

In addition to his elder brother John already mentioned, Robert Keith of Troup had a younger brother Alexander who married Marjorie Stewart, widow of John Dunbar earl of Moray. In 1391 William Keith, marischal, signed a charter which granted Alexander all the lands of Glencuthil in Buchan (Spalding Club, 1847, 380). Glencuthil, part of the lands of Aberdour, is immediately to the east of Troup in what later became Auchmedden. At this time, the rest of Aberdour was part of the wider Douglas lands (Brown, 1998, 267). In November 1402 Isabel, countess of Mar, granted the same Alexander Keith of Grandoun, the lordship of Glendowachy and the lands of Doune on the west side of

Troup (Spalding Club, 1847, 380); this grant was confirmed by King Robert III in 1403 at Dundonald.

Muriella, the oldest sister of Robert and Alexander Keith, had married Robert duke of Albany sometime after May 1380. By November 1403, Albany and Alexander Keith, his brother-in-law, were certainly in effective control of the barony of Kingedward to the south of Troup (Boardman, 1996, 253). One source says that Alexander Keith was in command of the cavalry at the battle of Harlaw in 1411. Albany and Muriella's second son, John Stewart, became earl of Buchan in 1406 and was granted Kingedward in 1415. In 1413 Alexander Keith granted to his daughter Christian and her husband Patrick Ogilvie of Auchterhouse the baronies of Doun and Grandoun, thereby introducing the Ogilvies north of the Mounth; Andrew Barclay was a witness to this grant.

Three points are worth noting. First, the Keiths, in addition to the specific examples above, also had lands further east and south in Buchan; it is fair to conclude that they did succeed at times in controlling large parts of the north-east, although changes could be frequent. Secondly, the Keiths, Barclays and Ogilvies were closely linked through marriage, though marital links do not necessarily imply shared interests and loyalties. Thirdly, as part of the need to allocate land to a growing number of family members, some landholdings were divided, sometimes temporarily; Glencuthil and Melrose illustrate this point. This will be a recurring theme.

This brief summary shows that the north-east was an area of particular interest to Keith family members. There are echoes of the Comyns in the extent of influence, the expansion of holdings and the means by which such expansion was achieved. It also illustrates the frequency of changes in land tenure in a relatively small geographical area.

At times, it seemed a good idea to record and collate all such changes across the wider area. However, that would undoubtedly have prolonged and complicated the research. Not only are the records incomplete, but the Keiths are not unique in having a complex family tree.

Alliances and Feuds

Another feature of this period, in the north-east as elsewhere, was the changing alliances and enmities between, and sometimes within, families. Although the reason for any feud or alliance did vary, a feature of many such incidents was the question of ownership and inheritance of land. Landholding represented wealth, and also potential power and influence; hence its pivotal importance. Some feuds lasted over a number of generations, with varying intensity. The Keiths as a major family, with ambitions and multiple landholdings and marital ties, were certainly not immune from participation in both feuds and alliances. One example was the extended 'cruel feud' between the Irvines of Drum and the Keiths which 'raged in the latter part of the fourteenth century' (Leith, 1909, 25). The sticking point, originally, appears to have been the inheritance of a surviving female, originally a Keith, who had married the laird of Drum, an Irvine. They jointly wished to claim her inheritance. The feud was finally settled in 1411, about the time of the battle of Harlaw, by the marriage of Elizabeth Keith, a daughter of Robert Keith who was the then Marischal (see next chapter), to Alexander Irvine of Drum. An important part of the settlement was the grant of the estates of Strachan as a dowry to the bride. The feud between the families was mentioned specifically in the marriage contract.

Drum Castle, family home of the Irvines of Drum, as it is today.

A second example from the same period involved the Keiths and the Lindsays. The critical background was the tension between Sir James Lindsay and the earl of Fife, a political ally of Marischal Keith (Boardman, 1996, 199). In 1395, Lindsay became involved in a feud with a Robert Keith. This seems to have been a serious matter as a pitched battle is recorded at Bourtrie in the Garioch. Lindsay was said to be leading a force of 400 men to relieve his wife, who was besieged in Lindsay's castle at Fyvie by Robert Keith. This is probably not the Robert Keith who inherited Troup but his nephew Robert, son of his elder brother John. To complicate matters further, the Robert Keith in question was said to be a nephew of Lindsay's wife.

Fyvie Castle as it is today.

The outcome was that Robert Keith and his adherents were defeated with the loss of about 60 men, and the siege was broken. This may have settled things down, for a time at least. This Robert Keith is probably the same one who appeared at an assize in Aberdeen in 1396/7 (NLS, Acc 6206, IV 5).

Similar events could be chosen to illustrate both positive and negative links with other families, such as Forbes or Gordon, with whom the Keiths also had marital links. Although such events are of interest in the wider story of the Keiths and are illustrative of aspects of life in that period in the north-east, they tend to draw the focus away from Troup, although specific examples relating to Troup will be given later.

To summarise, although the details are not always well-defined, the lordship of Troup passed from the de Trops to the Keiths in the latter half of the fourteenth century possibly in the 1370s, with a brief interlude of involvement of Andrew Buttergask. From being an estate occupied by a minor local family it became part of the landholdings of one of the most important and well-connected families in the north-east of Scotland whose head had a hereditary role in the royal court. It is now time to consider the Keiths of Troup in more detail.

8. KEITHS of TROUP

Robert Keith and John Keith

Sir Robert Keith, like a number of others who held the lands of Troup, does not appear often in the historical record. One important fact about him, on which there are differing views, is whether he was married once or twice, and which wife was the mother of the next Keith of Troup. Some assert that Robert and the Troup heiress had family; indeed Paul claims that the Troup heiress was the mother of all Robert's children, 3 sons and 4 daughters. Others believe that Robert's second wife (presumably after the death of his first wife) was Elizabeth Lindsay, daughter of David earl of Crawford and this union produced 3 sons and 2 daughters. At least there appears to be agreement on three sons, William, John and Alexander. As mentioned above, one daughter was Elizabeth.

Sir Robert Keith of Troup succeeded his father William as Marischal of Scotland, probably in 1408, the year he resigned his lands at Troup. Robert's eldest son, also William, was his designated heir and succeeded his father between July 1430 and May 1431; William was the Marischal who became the first Lord Keith. It is worth noting that for the years 1406-24, a substantial proportion of the time that Sir Robert Keith was Marischal, King James I was a prisoner in England. This must have impacted on the role of marischal in that period.

Sir Robert's second son, John, became the laird of Troup. While it may have happened earlier, it was confirmed in a charter in June 1413 (Spalding Club, 1843, 491). Given the feud between the Irvines of Drum and the Keiths, it is interesting to note that Alexander Irvine of Drum was one of the witnesses to the charter. In this charter, Robert reserved the superiority and service of free tenants of the lands of Achorthie, Curvie and Hayninghill, lying in the barony of Troup (Bannerman, 1897, 12). Achorthie in a later reference appears as Powistone, which is later renamed Gardenstown. Curvie is clearly Crovie. No reference to Hayninghill has been found but there are numerous references to Ha'hill at Pitgair to the south of present day Gardenstown; see the map in Pratt's Buchan in Appendix 1. It is the site of a motte and a ruin known as the Wallace Tower (Spence, 1873, 101). If that is correct, then the three areas are not conjoined but they do include 3 likely mottes in the area and, as a result, may have been the traditional seats of justice and so of particular interest to the feudal superior.

All the indications are that John Keith of Troup had a long life. A Keith family paper in the National Archives states that John's first wife was Margaret, a daughter of King Robert II. As no supporting evidence for this has been found. the statement should be judged doubtful, at best. John had three children, James, John and Eupham. At Eupham's marriage to Andrew Menzies of Durrisdeir, it is reported in a Keith family paper that John 'fell in love and afterwards married Eliza Menzies, sister of the said Andrew Menzies' by whom he had two further children, James Keith of Clackriach and Matilda who married Gilbert Abernethy (NAS, 1780, 36/308).

Despite his longevity the glimpses of John's life unfortunately are few. In June 1447 he was a witness to an instrument of transcript (NAS, 1780, GD 26/3/989). There is a reference in 1454 to a charter by him covering lands in Kincardineshire (Paul, 1909, 171). This suggests that some links between Troup and lands in Kincardine had been an enduring feature.

A feature of these years was a marked deterioration in the weather. For example, the winter of 1407/08 – when John Keith may have assumed the lands of Troup – was known as a 'great winter'. About the same time, cold easterly winds increased in frequency. Very cold winters also occurred in 1422, 1434 and 1437, famine followed in 1438. The pattern of poor weather, crop failures and famine years continued in the 1450s. Life at Troup, and indeed more widely in the north and east of Scotland, must have been very difficult in such conditions.

In 1462 an event of some significance occurred. John Keith of Troup resigned his whole estate of the lands and barony of Troup to his nephew William, who had succeeded his elder brother Robert (2nd Lord Keith) in 1446 and who became the first earl Marischal in 1458. At the same time John received for himself and his male heirs a new charter of the Ten Merk lands and barony of Northfield, part of the estate of Troup (see Appendix 1 for description).

Why did this happen? John Keith must have been over 75 years old by this time. He did have a male heir; indeed the claimed descent of the line of the Keiths of Northfield from John Keith to his son James and subsequent heirs into the eighteenth century is in papers in the National Archives (see Appendix 2).

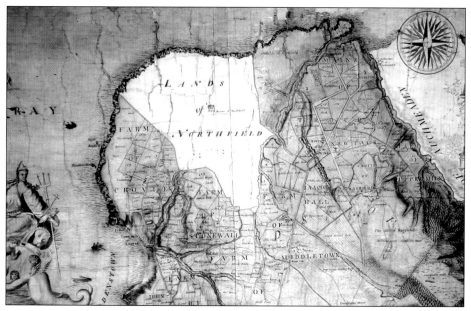

This is an edited portion of MS2676 showing the extent of the lands of Northfield in 1767. The plan was prepared by John Home. Note that the line of the coast where Troup Head and the immediate surrounding area should be is not drawn accurately, as the commission related to the survey of the lands of Troup.

Two possible factors may have prompted this course of action. The first, and potentially more influential, could have arisen from the need for the earl Marischal to put his affairs in order before his anticipated death; this was not an uncommon practice amongst the nobility. He did die before Whitsunday 1463; John Keith died before 1467. There had been no mention of Troup in the charter to Lord William Keith (grandfather of the earl Marischal in 1462) perhaps because Lord William at that point was 'incapable, from age or infirmity, of discharging his duties' (Innes, 1927, 288).

The second possibility is that the earl Marischal wished to ensure that Troup, in line with family tradition, remained a landholding to be allocated to a son of the earl Marischal. However, given that Troup was held by his uncle with perhaps the expectation that it would pass to the uncle's family, William earl Marischal, opted to allocate Northfield, a portion of the lands of Troup, effectively for his cousins to inherit, while retaining the lands and barony of Troup under more immediate control. He undertook a similar process with his niece Janet, only child of his elder brother Robert (Innes, 1927, 291). Again, this may indicate pressures to ensure that a growing number of relatives had landholdings.

John Keith now became the first Keith of Northfield (see Appendix 2), although he may have remained 'of Troup' until his death. Presumably at some point John Keith's family and heirs moved to Northfield. Whether the castle on Cullykhan remained occupied continuously is again pertinent. The next clear reference to Troup is in 1493 when there is a charter for the lands of Troup, confirmed in 1494 by James IV to William, second son of William 2nd earl Marischal, whose wife was Elizabeth Gordon daughter of George earl of Huntly (Paul, 1984, #2208). No evidence has been found that the 1st earl Marischal assigned Troup during the period 1462 until his death, probably in 1483; it does not seem likely that it remained unoccupied and unused.

Gilbert Keith of Troup

Further information on William Keith of Troup is limited. He was a witness to one of his father's charters at Dunottar, dated 3 March 1511. He was killed at Flodden on 9 September 1513. He had no children so, in accordance with the terms of the charter of 1493, he was succeeded by his next brother in line, Gilbert, who had originally been assigned Pittendrum by his father. Gilbert was in possession of it before 1511 but he resigned it on obtaining the barony of Troup (Paul, 1909, 44).

As with other Keiths of Troup, the facts of Gilbert's life are not agreed in the sources. Nor do many of the references shed much light on Gilbert and his actions. One source claims that Gilbert died in December 1537 reportedly with no issue but, in the same sentence, refers to a son George and a daughter Elizabeth! Another source mentions a son William. A third son, Alexander, has more convincing evidence than the others. Gilbert Keith is also mentioned in references in 1537 and 1552. In short, some caution is necessary, particularly in relation to lifespan and family, in relation to the Gilbert Keith references.

Looking at the family first, two women, Elizabeth Forbes and Isobel (or Isabel) Forbes who are sisters, are mentioned as wives. Chronologically the references to wives – Elizabeth in 1525 and Isabel in 1527 and 1532 –

allow for two marriages and one source specifically states that Gilbert Keith 'afterwards married another of Lord Forbes' daughters' (Tayler & Tayler, 1937, 62-3). However, this last quote is in the context of Gilbert Keith being a witness at a court case in February 1529; this does not sit easily with the others who suggest that a second marriage took place between 1525 and May 1527. Such confusion about names or dates is all too common in such circumstances.

The Forbes family would probably have been well known to the Keiths of Troup. John 6th Lord Forbes, the father of both Elizabeth and Isobel, was given permission by James IV in 1509 to construct a new castle or tower at Kingedward, a project which did not proceed. This was near the Forbes' lands of Blacktown in the barony of Kingedward, not far from the likely boundary with Troup. On balance, although there may be uncertainty about dates, it is likely that Gilbert Keith married in turn Elizabeth Forbes and her sister Isabel.

One of the references to Isabel Forbes also includes the only reference to a son William, which of course is a very plausible name for a male member of the Keith family in the early sixteenth century. There is also a single reference to George (Paul, 1907, 44) which adds that George was still a minor in 1553. The same reference lists a daughter Elizabeth who, in 1550, was contracted to marry George Baird, second son of Andrew Baird of Auchmedden (Grant, 1922, 490; Bulloch, 1934, 180). Given the date here, it is pertinent to note that Bulloch states that Baird and his son Gilbert were ardent Catholics: indeed Gilbert is called a 'rigid papist', who was fined for not attending the kirk. George Baird's affiliation is further witnessed when he attended the Earl of Huntly at the battle of Corrichie in 1562; he was also said to be present at an 'insurrection in Aberdeen' in 1589 on the Roman Catholic side.

Considering all the above, it seems that Gilbert Keith did have children, probably 2 daughters and perhaps 3 sons. The date of 1537 for his demise is probably not correct but no other date has been found. This will be considered below in the question of the succession.

Many of the references found for Gilbert Keith are associated with charter or land references. On four occasions - 1521, 1530, 1537 and 1552 - he is cited as a witness to a charter. Before looking at one undated reference, the others, listed in chronological order, are:

1525 The teind share of the church of St Fergus held by the laird of Inverugy (another Keith, of course) was leased to Gilbert Keith of Troup and Elizabeth Forbes, his wife (Cheyne, undated).

1527 (May) There was an Instrument of Assignation by Gilbert Keith of Troup in favour of Isabel Forbes, his wife, of £100 Scots (NAS, GD 57/1/133A). Could this be connected to their marriage?

1529 (February) At Aberdeen, Gilbert Keith of Troup was a witness to a pact 'of mutual agreement to keep the peace' in a case between William Leslie of Balquhand and John Lord Forbes, his father in law (Taylor, 1937, 62).

1532 Gilbert and Isobel, together with their son William, were given a tack of land in the sheriffdom of Kincardine by John, Abbot of Lindores (NAS, GD 49/30).

1537 As part of the assize of perambulation referred to earlier in connection with Lethnot, Gilbert Keith is recorded as holding the lands of Troup under William, earl Marischal.

1550 Elizabeth Keith, daughter of Gilbert Keith of Troup, married George Baird of Auchmedden.

Gilbert Keith appears to have been laird of Troup for a lengthy period. Such tenure could imply a degree of stability. It is possible also to see improved circumstances because of links to the Gordons. Could such factors have created the conditions where further developments were made to the castle at Troup?

Links to the Gordons and to Masons' Marks

The undated reference to Gilbert Keith provides the basis for suggesting the link to castle improvement. Gilbert Keith is recorded as the tutor of his nephew William, son of his elder brother Robert, who became the third earl Marischal (Paul, 1907, 46). Given that William was still a minor in 1525, it is likely that this was happening in the 1520s. The implication surely is that Gilbert Keith himself must have been a person of some education before being entrusted with such a responsibility. It is valid to consider whether he also tutored William's sister Elizabeth. In 1535 she married George Gordon 4th earl of Huntly. Elizabeth Keith is cited (Sanderson, 2002, 143) as being provided with an education that, unusually for women at that time, included writing.

One of the most striking features uncovered in the excavation of the Castle Site at Cullykhan was the fallen arch in the kitchen where there are two examples of the same mason's mark. While structurally the arch has similarities to others, for example at Edzell Castle, the same mason's mark has been found at Huntly Castle. The acknowledged date of completion of this part of the building at Huntly is 1553. Associated with this phase at Huntly are George Gordon 4th earl and Elizabeth Keith, mentioned above (Simpson, 1922, 139). There are other contacts and links between Gordons and Keiths. A date in the 1550s would fit the redevelopment of the kitchen at Troup as well as Huntly Castle.

The mark has also been identified at Delgatie Castle, where work was begun by the 8th laird, Alexander Hay, around 1550 and continued by his

The kitchen fireplace arch is shown after the initial clearance of the surrounding kitchen area. The arch stones are as they fell or slumped indicating a wholesale collapse of the arch. Careful examination showed that it was close to its original position.

This close-up photo showing the mason's mark was taken in the course of excavation soon after the arch was found.

The kitchen fireplace arch at Edzell Castle in Angus is no longer in situ. Its current setting on the ground in the castle helps to indicate similarities with the Cullykhan arch. There are no mason's marks on the arch stones at Edzell but there are numerous marks in the castle. No matches for the mark at Troup were found.

Huntly Castle remains a fine example of Scottish architecture. The first match for the mason's mark was found here.

son William into the 1560s (Innes, 1936, 32). There is also a potentially relevant link between Janet Forbes, another daughter of John 6th lord Forbes and thus a sister-in-law of Gilbert Keith, who, after the death of her first husband, the earl of Atholl, married Alexander Hay of Delgatie, the 5th laird, c.1545. Another example of the mark is at Pluscarden Abbey where a similar date applies for its location in the Dunbar Vestry. While masons' marks do not provide definitive dating evidence, the coincidence of the marks and the linkages described here may support the dating of the kitchen arch at Cullykhan to the early 1550s.

The Later Keiths of Troup

The details of the succession after Gilbert Keith are uncertain. One reference indicates that 'by the kindness of the earl Marischal' the widow of Gilbert Keith of Troup had the gift of the lands of Troup for 'herself and her bairns' for ten years after the death of Gilbert (Tayler and Tayler, 1937, 58). No date is associated with this. The name of the widow is given as Elizabeth Forbes; is this a third wife or an inconsistency in the sources?

Certainly, Alexander Keith had inherited by 1 August 1577 (NAS, RH6/2445). This reference is significant for a number of reasons. First, because it concerns an agreement between Alexander Keith of Troup and Patrick Cheyne of Esselmont and statements in it about Alexander Keith are likely to be accurate. It makes reference to the 1537 perambulation of Lethnot between Gilbert Keith, 'Alexander's father', and Patrick Cheyne, grandfather of the person signing in 1577. Second, Alexander Keith clearly has inherited Troup by the date of the agreement. Third, it is written at Troup so Alexander Keith is in residence there and the castle is probably still in use. It appears that Alexander succeeded his father, although it is possible that an older brother, William, may have been laird of Troup first, but it should be stressed that there is no evidence to support this.

In 1580, Alexander Keith was designated a burgess of Aberdeen but not to hold property therein (New Spalding Club, 1890, 75). No other details of Alexander's activities are known, but some information about his family can be pieced together from a variety of sources. He had at least 2 sons and 3 daughters, though the name of his wife is unknown. His older son John succeeded, at least by 1587. A second son Robert is also recorded as a burgess of Aberdeen in 1596 (New Spalding Club, 1890, 88). Elizabeth was probably the oldest daughter. In 1577 she married John

Keith, brother of George who succeeded his grandfather to become fourth earl Marischal in 1589. A second daughter Marjory married John Keith of Northfield. The third daughter Barbara married William Keith of Pittendrum in 1581, a 'distant cousin' who died in 1590. The phrase 'keeping it in the family' seems appropriate.

As indicated above John Keith, elder son of Alexander Keith of Troup, was fiar of Troup in 1587 (Bulloch, 1903, 204), the same year that King James VI, at Falkland, confirmed a charter to George earl Marischal which included Troup with castles, houses, mills, woods, fishing etc. The name of one daughter Isobel is known; between 1587 and 1592 she married George Gordon. John Keith is mentioned in a charter of 1592 as third in line of succession to George, earl Marischal.

John Keith appears to have been associated with a number of incidents. In 1587, William Gordon of Gight was bound over not to harm John Keith, fiar of Troup, and his tenants of the lands of Cairnbannoch

George Keith, 4th earl Marischal and head of the Keith family, was the founder of Marischal College in Aberdeen.

and was subject to a caution of £2,000 by Sir George Ogilvie of Dunlugas. Whether this is linked to the report of a tryst (possibly arranged as part of a process of arbitration to settle a dispute), in 1587 in Aberdeen, between the earl of Huntly, the most powerful figure in north-east Scotland, and the earl Marischal which ended in a fight and with the slaughter of a Keith gentleman, John Keith of Claikriach, by William Gordon of Gight is not clear (Brown, 1986, 51).

This was a period of considerable violence in Scottish society. The enhanced availability of hand-held arms such as pistols was surely a contributory factor. 'Arms were owned and carried by most men, and even minor arguments could assume very dangerous proportions.' There seems to have been no shortage of pretexts for disputes over issues such as fishing rights, supply of peats, and, predominantly, land boundaries and inheritance. There is reference to the 'violent tendencies of John

Gordon of Gight and his young friends' in groups such as 'The Knights of Mortar' (Brown, 1986, 20).

Keiths, Gordons and Aberdeen

Marital links between the Keiths and the Gordons, mentioned above, may represent a high point in the relations between the main branches of the respective families. However, that perception must be viewed alongside the known differences in the important matter of religion.

It is well known that, during the Reformation, the Gordons were strongly pro-Catholic. This was not the case with the Keiths, at least as far as the heads of the family were concerned. William Keith, the 3rd earl Marischal, who had converted to Protestantism in 1544, was a supporter of George Wishart (burnt at the stake in St Andrews for his reformist teaching) and 'appears to have been a highly religious man'. This religious stance was continued by his successor as earl Marischal, George Keith. Indeed he 'presented himself as the staunchly Protestant champion of the North East' (Kerr-Petersen, 2016, 99). This was a potential source of friction with the Gordons, one shared by other families with links to the Gordons.

One area of rivalry between the families was their relative status in the burgh of Aberdeen. The Gordons' 'monopoly' on the post of provost of Aberdeen was challenged in the 1580s and overturned in 1593 with the election of John Cheyn, a client of William Keith, the fifth earl Marischal. Given that this was also when Marischal College was founded, it is a tangible indicator of the growing wealth and influence of the Keiths in the city of Aberdeen. The Mackintosh raid in 1589 on Keith lands in the Mearns, at the instigation of Huntly, also displays a competitive rather than amicable relationship (Robertson, 2011, 32).

Overall, it seems that differences, in religious views and other matters, existed between the earl of Huntly, as head of the Gordon family, and the earl Marischal, as head of the Keiths. The continuing, and possibly escalating, difficulties arising from such differences, would surely have dominated the relationship between the families. Although no direct evidence has been found, it would be surprising, and unusual, if branches of the families, such as the Keiths of Troup, were not fully attuned to these differences, even if they may not have been active in particular disputes.

Similar links apply between the Keiths, including Keith of Troup, and the Forbes family. Members of the Gordon family are also involved in the story. A well documented feud between the Gordons and the Forbes which had culminated in 1571 in a decisive defeat of a substantial Forbes-led force included 'the son of the earl Marischal' (Potter, 2002, 99). Sons of the earl Marischal (William master of Marischal, and John) were identified as leading figures in the Forbes group. However the group split, deliberately, near Aberdeen with John Keith heading north - whether his brother was still with either group is unclear - while the others, under the master of Forbes, turned east towards Aberdeen where, on 20 November, they were soundly beaten with 300 killed and 200 taken prisoner. The leader of the victorious forces at Aberdeen, Adam Gordon, was a cousin of the earl Marischal; their mothers were sisters.

These glimpses serve to illustrate the complexity of events and the connections between some of the people involved in what was undoubtedly a turbulent period. Families would focus very much on their own perceived interests, forming 'alliances' when appropriate or convenient.

John Keith of Troup and the Privy Council

The sparse records do not show whether any Keiths from Troup were active participants in the events; described above. There is some evidence, however, which showed that the wider trends in society at the end of the sixteenth century also made their mark at Troup.

John Keith of Troup was an aggrieved party in 1587. However, he was the subject of a number of complaints to the Privy Council in 1589, 1594 and 1602. In the first case, an unspecified 'accident' between Patrick Cheyne of Essilmonth and John Keith of Troup led to £2000 cautions against both of them (Masson, 1881, 402).

In the second case, John Chene, portioner of Cruvie, complains against John Keith and Gilbert Baird of Auchmeden, who possibly lived at Auchmeden Castle. There is an echo of much earlier events in this story in John Chene's statement of complaint in the Register of the Privy Council. He described how John Keith, and his accomplices, with long guns, swords, spears and other prohibited weapons, came to his half lands of Cruvie. Alerted, John Chene managed to make his escape. Seeing this, Keith was sufficiently incensed to wound the complainer's tenants and servants, demolish his house and eject his wife and bairns; then he 'maist cruellie and unmercifullie' rode over Elspeth Maitland (Chene's wife) with horses who, in addition to injuries all over her body, suffered a miscarriage; at the time of the complaint she was still bed-ridden and in danger of her life. As the complainer was present in person and the defender was not, the latter was denounced rebel (Masson, 1882, 129).

In the final case, James Cheyne of Pennan complained about the same two individuals for raids on Pennan. The twelve complaints in this case cover the period from 1594, when Gilbert Baird was accused of killing James Cheyne's horse. In 1597, when Baird accompanied by John Keith with 'certaine notorious murtherers and treasonable fyre-raisers… (including) Alexander Keith, George Keyth… and others to the number of 60 persons' came to Cheyne's place and besieged him and his family shooting pistolets at the windows and doors. Undoubtedly the most serious of the complaints was that Gilbert Baird, with John Keith and others, passed to the lands of Fintry and murdered Gilbert Kirkpatrick; having 'dowkit and dippit' a piece of linen in the said Gilbert's blood, it was placed on top of the Laird of Troup's (John Keith) own house. It should be noted that such a display on Cullykhan would be clearly visible from Pennan and surroundings.

This view is taken from the foreshore at the village of Pennan looking at Cullykhan with the greater mass of Lion's Head protruding behind. The top of Hell's Lum is just visible in Lion's Head. The castle on Cullykhan would have been a landmark from this, and other, directions, even more with a blood-stained linen cloth waving in the wind.

This time the pursuer and defender both appeared. In the majority of the complaints, the judgement was that the pursuer had not proved his case. The other points, including the latter two, were referred to the Justice for decision (Masson, 1884, 360). No detail of any subsequent action has been found.

If these events are indicative, then life at that time was certainly difficult and fraught with danger, with violence all too frequently used as a means of resolving problems. There is also evidence that food may not have been plentiful because of poor harvests, principally due to bad weather. Extracting a living from lands in the Troup area may have become more challenging than formerly and may have been a contributory factor to simmering tensions and disputes.

These events may also serve as a harbinger of financial difficulties. Payment of fines may have been an issue. A wadset for 8,000 merks was signed in December 1600 by the earl Marischal over the lands of Troup. By 1610 Gilbert Keith, probably a son of John, had succeeded to Troup as the wadset was discharged in his favour in that year (New Spalding Club, 1906, 159). This may be the last of the line of Keiths as the next reference (Ferguson, 1913, 227) is to the grant of the lands of Troup in 1632 to Sir James Gordon of Lesmoir.

The End of Occupation of the Castle

There is no clear date for the initial construction of the castle. Its abandonment and demise as a habitation also go unremarked in the record, until the reference by Gordon of Straloch, at an unspecified date, that the castle was 'neglected'. Just as an approximate date for its construction may be deduced from fragmentary written evidence, so may a date range for its abandonment be inferred.

First, no reference to a Keith of Troup has been found with a date later than 1610. Is the Gilbert Keith mentioned there the last of the Keiths of Troup? Does it indicate that the estate passed to another family? This raises a question about the whereabouts of the Keith place of residence. Given that Alexander Keith and one of his sons were burgesses in Aberdeen, does that point to Aberdeen becoming the location of the family residence, matching the focus of the earl Marischal?

Changes are recorded which pertain to both the lands of Troup and Northfield about this time. There is a charter of 1630 to Sir William Keith of Ludqharn, and his eldest lawful son, also William, for the Ten Merk Lands of Northfield and part of Quyhtfeild, previously part of Mains of Troup, on the resignation of William, earl Marischal. In 1632, the King granted to Sir James Gordon of Lesmoir the lands and barony of Troup. Bulloch in his book on the House of Gordon suggests that the barony of Troup, granted to Sir William Keith of Ludqharn, had reverted to the earl Marischal's family, and was re-granted (Bulloch, 1907, 47). Further evidence supporting this highlights William Keith of Ludqharn having financial difficulties and losing a large part of his estates 'at the instance of the earl Marischal' (Tayler & Tayler, 1933, 205)

In 1654 the Gardens acquired Troup when Major Alexander Garden, who had served in Germany under Gustavus Adolphus of Sweden, returned to Scotland and purchased the estate (Grant, 1922, 31). For his residence he built the first Troup House, which was not on Cullykhan. The Castle Site may have served as a useful quarry. However Aberdeenshire Council's site record describes this Troup House as 'a modest two-storied house of large clay bricks', which is more flattering than the description of it in *The Northern Farmer* in May 1897, 'a mud house of two stories'. For the second Troup House, built either in 1763 or 1772, one description is that it was 'entirely constructed of massive red sandstone blocks' which originated, not on Cullykhan, but from a quarry on the Law Hill of Crovie (Smith, 1964, 54). Certainly Douglas in 1782 describes it as a modern building, three storeys high and very substantially built (Douglas, 1782, 290).

Another dimension to explore in connection with the end of occupation of the castle is the physical state of the castle building. Reference was made earlier to extensive slippage from the Castle Site visible both from the excavated area, particularly near the kitchen, and on the shore below. The last phase of building was the improved and expanded kitchen area which, given the quality of what remained, was clearly substantial. It must, too, have extended close to the cliff edge. A major collapse or slippage over the cliff is likely, given the evidence. A significant collapse would mean that the castle was without a viable kitchen and lacking drainage facilities. The possibility of further damage would also be a concern. In such circumstances, it is doubtful whether the

These three pictures provide complementary perspectives on the issues of collapse and slippage in the context of the abandonment of the castle on Cullykhan.

The first shows the line of the extensive rock fault, almost certainly the underlying cause. The photo shows the emergence of the Needle's E'e into the Devil's Kitchen with the line of the fault, extending up the cliff, directly under the site of the castle.

The second was taken during the excavation of the kitchen area on the Castle Site. The key point here is how the left side of the castle has been, and is being, lost over the side of the cliff towards the beach in Cullykhan Bay. This is the opposite

side of the headland from the first picture and indicates that substantial loss and erosion took place on both sides.

The final picture is taken from Lion's Head looking across Cullykhan with Pennan in the distance. The Mill Shore at Nethermill (the 'mouth' of the Tore of Troup) is also visible. The critical aspect is the rock on the side of Cullykhan facing the viewer. Both above the Devil's Kitchen (to the right) and below Fort Fiddes (to the left) are large-scale rock falls/slippage/collapse. These removed some of the castle outbuildings, as well as leaving parts of the ramparts of Fort Fiddes perilously close to joining them at the foot of the cliff.

castle would have remained safe and habitable. A prompt abandonment seems quite likely.

A number of scenarios could be conjectured. However, putting all of the above together there is an argument for thinking the castle was abandoned as uninhabitable in the early part of the seventeenth century, probably before the changes initiated by the charters around 1630.

In terms of the story of the castle on Cullykhan, this is a convenient point to halt. It is noteworthy however, that there is a family connection between the Gardens and the Keiths. George Garden, who became Laird of Banchory in 1555, married Isobel Keith, daughter of the Laird of Troup, about 1548 (Spalding Club, 1852, 326). The likelihood is that she was another daughter of Gilbert Keith and his wife Isobel. The great-grandson of George and Isobel was Major Alexander Garden, 1st Laird of Troup; yet another example of the connections between families in the north-east.

Like the de Trops before them, the final details of the last Keith of Troup can only be inferred from glimpses of people and events. It is reasonable to conclude that by the mid 1600s the power, wealth and prestige of the Keiths was past its peak in the north-east; the known events concerning Troup support that view. If the collapse of parts of the castle due to slippage was the main cause of its abandonment, then the end may have been sudden rather than prolonged. We may never know.

The castle did not represent the final use of the site. To the seaward side of the castle site is a flat area which was said to have been a bowling green at an uncertain date, generally thought to be in the late seventeenth or early eighteenth century. Beyond this are the ramparts of Fort Fiddes, which must now be considered.

9. FORT FIDDES RECONSIDERED

Searching for Fort Fiddes

The principal focus of this research has always been the historical period prior to the acquisition of Troup by Major Garden in 1654, but at times the wish to round off the story of what happened on Cullykhan has prompted a search for more information about the fort and Captain Fiddes, after whom it was said to be named. The hope was that, being more recent, records were likely to be easier to find and more extensive. The search was not straightforward, often frustrating, and, not infrequently, put aside as a problem whose solution would not be found. Ultimately a range of literary, documentary and cartographic sources proved enlightening. New evidence, not available at the time of previous publications on the site, provides a convincing date for the construction of the fort, its purpose, and the key people involved.

To recap, the date generally ascribed to Fort Fiddes was approximately 1680. How did this date come to be accepted? One likely source is a paper on the Gardens of Troup by J Wilson Smith published in the Transactions of the Buchan Field Club in 1964, following a talk he gave to the Club in September 1959. The proximity of the date of

This photograph was published in Grampian's Past: Its Archaeology from the Air by Ian A G Shepherd & Moira K Greig in 1996. It shows many features on Cullykhan. It is included here because it provides the best illustration of the line of the ramparts of Fort Fiddes, at the top of the picture.

this publication to the beginning of the excavations on the site may be significant.

The principal evidence advanced to support the 1680 date was an estate plan of Troup, attributed to John Ray and dated 1707, a copy of which was included in the first publication on the excavations (Greig, 1970, 275). Whether the date of 1707 was on the original of the plan or notified to Mr Smith is not clear. Attempts to clarify this point have been unsuccessful.

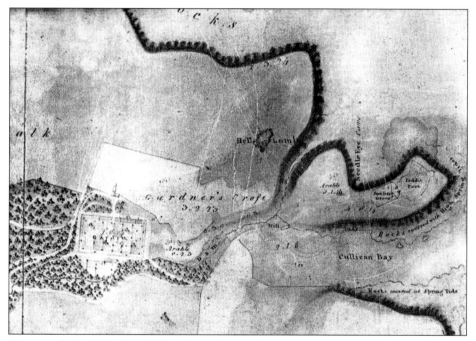

A copy of the John Ray's Plan from Colvin Greig's 1971 Report in the Aberdeen University Review.

It is possible to find some evidence to support a date of 1680 for the fort. There were documented concerns in the area about hostile French naval activity, described sometimes as privateers under French colours. A good example of this, essentially piratical, action is given in the Seafield Correspondence in a letter dated 12 June 1698 from three baillies of Banff to Sir James Ogilvie which tells of the capture, in Gamrie Bay, of the ship of one Wm Hay, en route to the Spey for food (Grant J, 1912, 104).

It is known, too, that the then Garden of Troup was active in a local Militia in 1688 (Grant J, 1912, 219). However, none of this supporting evidence is conclusive. There are other instances of concerns about possible French invasion which do not support a date of 1680. A Banffshire Field Club paper of 1908 commemorates, with an extensive description, the events of March 1708 under the title *The French Invasion of Scotland Two Hundred Years Ago*.

It seemed clear that the greatest reliance for a date of 1680 for Fort Fiddes was placed on John Ray's map dated 1707. Other doubts began to emerge. Initial searches for a Captain Fiddes, a portrait of whom had hung in Troup House in the 1960s, and had been seen by some diggers, only found evidence of a potential fort-builder in Gambia and Barbados, in the last decade of the eighteenth century. The portrait also seemed to have disappeared.

No copy of John Ray's plan has been located. Extensive searches have provided no trace of a surveyor called John Ray. That in itself is not conclusive. However, the style of the plan is indicative of a later date, at least post 1760; on these grounds alone the earlier date is questionable.

A stronger pointer emerged from an estate map of Troup prepared by John Home (Archives of the University of Aberdeen, MS2626) which can be securely dated to 1767. This shows no evidence of Fort Fiddes on Cullykhan, which is called Castle Hill. John Home is well-known as a surveyor through his mapping of Assynt. Why is there no indication of Fort Fiddes on Home's map? By this point, the unsuccessful search for information about the fort, its construction and the elusive Captain Fiddes (or his portrait) was increasingly indicating that the answer to the question was that it did not exist in 1767.

The Story of Fort Fiddes – At Last!

It is now possible to state, on the basis of a range of historical sources, that the date for completion of Fort Fiddes was 1803.

The first lead was provided in a book called *Bonnet Lairds* by Giles Thornton-Kemsley, published in 1972. This is a history of the Thornton estate south of Laurencekirk, in the Mearns. The connection to Troup is Francis Garden, Lord Gardenstone, who was the 26th Laird of Thornton from 1786 to 1793, as well as Laird of Troup. He also had the estate of Johnston which bordered Thornton.

He had inherited Troup from his elder brother Alexander Garden in 1785. Alexander Garden was MP for Aberdeenshire and had erected a mansion house on the Troup estate in 1772. It is said that Lord Gardenstone inherited a rental roll of £30,000 and a personal fortune of £40,000.

Lord Gardenstone, a famous judge, was strongly committed to the development of Laurencekirk. Further information about him can be found in the papers on the Gardens of Troup and in John Kay's publication of 1838 which, in addition to being a fascinating biographical account, includes a sketch showing Lord Gardenstone on his way to work. He was succeeded in both estates by his nephew Francis Garden of Troup in 1793. Francis's father was Peter Garden of Delgaty, a younger brother of Lord Gardenstone.

Lord Gardenstone (Francis Garden 1721-93), shown en route from his house in Morningside to the Court, where he was a well-known judge, accompanied by his favourite dog Smash, and followed by a Highland boy whose duty it was to take charge of his horse after arrival at Parliament House.

According to *Bonnet Lairds*, the later Francis Garden is the man responsible for the construction of Fort Fiddes. Garden's background was in the military - he was a Captain in the 53rd Foot - and after his return to Banffshire he was appointed Major in the Sixth (Aberdeenshire) Regiment of Militia in Scotland, and a Deputy Lord Lieutenant of Banffshire in 1798. He took this responsibility seriously and "applied himself zealously" to preparation for defence against threatened invasion by Napoleon Bonaparte. The Lord Lieutenant of Banffshire, Lord Fife, had proposed the creation of alarm stations at six points along the coast. The National Map Library has a reference to a survey by the Board of Ordnance at Banff in the 1790s. It is also relevant to note the installation on the Battery Green at Banff in 1803 - perhaps the result of the survey mentioned above - of two 18-pounder and four 12-pounder guns 'through the fear of enemy attack'. However the only known construction took place at Troup by Francis Garden 'who had a fort constructed on his property at a place called Fort Fiddes' (Thornton-Kemsley, 1972, 111 – 120).

Correspondence re Fort Fiddes

Documentary evidence to support this statement can be found in the Montcoffer Papers where the details of the correspondence between Francis Garden of Troup, Lord Fife, and others about the fort remain. Writing to Lord Fife from Troup House in June 1804, Garden reported that the fort erected at his own expense had been inspected and approved by Major General the Marquis of Huntly. Ammunition having been provided for it, he suggested that it would be prudent to have it manned, to which end he offered to raise The Banff Battery Company by the forty men necessary to bring it to establishment strength and to recommend an officer to command the detachment. Lord Fife regarded this proposal favourably. He forwarded Garden of Troup's letter to Lord Moira, who in 1803 had been appointed commander-in-chief in Scotland, to seek his

support. If such support was forthcoming, he asked that Lord Moira forward both Mr Garden's letter and Lord Fife's accompanying letter to Lord Hawkesbury, the recently appointed Home Secretary, for approval. In his letter Lord Fife recommended this patriotic proposal, saying that Mr Garden's 'exertions for the protection

Lord Moira was born as Francis Rawden in 1754 in County Down. He added Hastings to his surname in 1789 when his mother succeeded to the barony of Hastings. He succeeded his father as Earl of Moira in 1793. In 1803 he was appointed commander-in-chief in Scotland. Later he was Governor-General in India, and was raised to be the first Marquess of Hastings in 1817 for his distinguished service there.

of this part of the coast' had been 'very spirted' and that the fort was in a situation 'well calculated to annoy an enemy; it commanded a bay in which trading vessels would be apt to run for protection from privateers'. To meet the defenceless condition of the coast Lord Fife proposed the recruitment of Sea Fencibles. The original of Francis Garden's letter may still be in the National Archives at Kew. However, its terms are clear from the copy correspondence in the Aberdeen University Archives.

The terms of Lord Hawkesbury's answer, together with the original of Francis Garden's letter to Lord Fife which shows his displeasure at the terms of the response, are still in the Aberdeen University Archives. Briefly, Lord Hawkesbury did not support the proposal in a way that found favour with Mr Garden.

Robert Jenkinson, Lord Hawkesbury, later Earl of Liverpool. Born in 1770, he became Lord Hawkesbury in 1796 when his father became 1st Earl of Liverpool. He was Foreign and Home Secretary. He succeeded to the title Lord Liverpool in 1808. He became Prime Minister, and remained so until 1827. He died in 1828.

As Mr Garden indicated in his reply to Lord Fife, dated 19 July 1804, he regretted 'exceedingly His Lordship (i.e. Hawkesbury) recommends the system of 3 August 1803 – a system under which no consideration on Earth could make me undertake any number of Volunteers as it would distress myself, without being of the smallest use to my <u>King</u> & <u>Country</u>!!!' His view was that volunteers could not be relied upon, 'men who only attend <u>when they think proper</u>, and <u>when they are pleased to attend</u>'. As a former officer, Mr Garden could not countenance this way of organising the defence of the realm. He was 'certain your Lordship' (Fife) would agree that a better idea was to 'half man the Fort with his own servants and labourers, when required' even if it 'should cost me a little money' rather than 'lie playing at soldiers'.

Lord Fife seemed willing to accept Lord Hawkesbury's view and asked Mr Garden if he would forward a more measured response to Lord Hawkesbury. A response from Mr Garden, without excessive underlinings and exclamation marks, was received by return. This letter also contained the suggestion that Lord Fife 'give yourself no further trouble', a view Lord Fife accepted in his subsequent letter of 20 July to Lord Hawkesbury. Perhaps Lord Fife was better attuned or connected politically, or wished to be. As an aside, Lord Hawkesbury became the 2nd Earl of Liverpool, and was appointed Prime Minister in 1812.

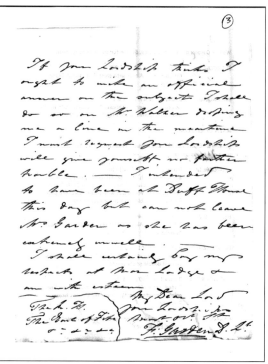

This is an example of a page in Francis Garden's handwriting, with his signature, from Troup House in 1804.

This correspondence, some of it in Francis Garden's own handwriting, provides direct evidence of the date of the construction of the fort in 1803. Francis Garden had a leading role in that. He had fulfilled his duty as a Major in the Aberdeenshire Militia. However, there is no mention of Captain Fiddes.

Captain Fiddes

I am grateful to Ed Knipe for sharing information on a further source which supports the account above, and also provides a range of biographical detail about Captain James Fiddes. The information comes from the *Personal Memoirs of Pryse Lockhart Gordon*, published in London in 1830. Gordon devotes approximately 20 pages to Jamie Fiddes, as he was known, providing interesting insights into his character and career, not all of which are relevant to the story of Troup.

Pryse Lockhart Gordon as he appears in the frontispiece of his published 1830 Journal.

Fiddes was the son of a dyer in Aberdeen; he and Gordon were at College together and became good friends whose paths crossed intermittently thereafter. Fiddes had been 'severely handled by the small-pox' when young which contributed to the 'oddity' of his facial appearance; it put one observer 'in mind of the heel of a darned stocking'. Apparently Fiddes did not find such comments untoward or upsetting. Fiddes studied land surveying as apprentice to a clever Englishman 'whom Lord Findlater had brought to Cullen House to survey his estates'. Later he was recommended by Lord Adam Gordon, the parliamentary representative for Kincardineshire and resident of The Burn near Edzell, to Lord Townsend, the master-general of the Ordnance, who met him more than once and regarded him favourably. Indeed it is said that Lord Townsend, a talented artist in his own right, drew a caricature of Fiddes which Fiddes much enjoyed.

After a probationary period, Fiddes was commissioned in the Royal Engineers with promotions listed in the London Gazette in 1793. In 1796 he was made Captain. During this period, it is noted, Fiddes retained his Aberdeen accent; he was also known for his good humour and musical ability as a flute player.

In his memoirs, Gordon writes that around 1790 Fiddes served in Barbados where a Lieutenant Fiddes was involved in work at St Ann's Castle, a coastal fort (National Archives, MPHH 1/100). Gordon does not confirm another reference to a Royal Engineer Fiddes surveying overseas. In December 1783 a Lieutenant James Fiddes surveyed the entrance of the river Gambia for occupation and fort construction. This may be the same Lieutenant Fiddes (National Archives, MPG 1/222, 1/223).

When Gordon encountered him in Barbados, Fiddes had acquired 'great reputation as an engineer', but 'the habits of the country had made him a sot'. His developing alcohol addiction led to Fiddes being recalled to

Britain. Ultimately, despite the continuing support of Lord Townsend, he was retired from the Engineers on 1 July 1799 as no longer fit for duty as confirmed in the London Gazette. Thereafter Fiddes returned to Aberdeenshire.

Gordon was a 'particular friend' of Mr Garden of Troup who 'had been long meditating to fortify a neck of land near his house in Banffshire'. Gordon recommended Fiddes for employment in the design and construction of the planned fort. He also gave advice to Mr Garden about Fiddes's 'diet-drink' while he was resident at Troup House, advice which seems to have been heeded. The work went ahead and produced 'a most scientific and beautiful little fortress, embracing every inch of the ground'. On his return to Aberdeen, Fiddes could not maintain 'the sobriety he had practised at Troup' and not long after died. The costs of his funeral were met by the Marquis of Huntly and Mr. Garden of Troup.

Two More Notes

Further confirmation of this timescale for the fort is given in a report in *The Scots Magazine* of March 1804 where under 'Affairs in Scotland' it reads.

A battery has lately been erected by Mr Garden of Troup on Coulie-cann …. It embraces under its protection the whole range of the Bays of Troup and Auchmeden, so that coasting vessels …. find shelter and safety from the attacks of privateers, or other vessels of the enemy. …. While it reflects much honour on the public spirit of Mr Garden, who has raised this necessary means of defence in a quarter where it was much wanted, it does no less credit to the professional abilities of Captain Fiddes of the Engineers, who has in its contrivance and execution given evident proofs of his science and good taste. Mr Garden has, in consequence of the satisfaction that this work afforded him, given the battery the appropriate name of Fort Fiddes.

All of the above supports the information entry for Fort Fiddes in the Ordnance Survey Name Book in 1868 that it is a 'fort, erected during the last war with France by the then proprietor of Troup, and situated on a rocky promontory on the north side of Cullykhan shore'.

In Conclusion

The documentary evidence for Fort Fiddes being built in 1803 is overwhelming. The sources quoted provide the context for its construction; how the instigator, Francis Garden of Troup, and the engineer, Captain James Fiddes formerly of the Royal Engineers, were involved. The remains of Fort Fiddes may still be seen today on Cullykhan.

John Ray's map cannot be dated 1707. It must be after 1803; is it 1807 rather than 1707? The absence of the Fort on John Home's map is explained. A later plan of Troup, prepared in 1826 by Walker & Beattie of Aberdeen, clearly shows a Battery on the site of Fort Fiddes (Aberdeenshire Archives, DD 21/1/47). Perhaps the Bowling Green marked on John Ray's plan is a Battery Green. Interestingly, Smith of the Buchan Field Club also mentions a Battery Green. For those who have experienced even summer weather on Cullykhan it would be no surprise to learn that there never was a bowling green there.

Reference has been made to a portrait of Captain Fiddes in Troup House. As well as having been seen by several diggers from the excavation site, it was also mentioned by Smith in his paper in 1964. He had seen the portrait, and refers to Fiddes, in the portrait, as a "little, snub-nosed, assertive soldier".

In the Collection of the Royal Engineers Museum, Library and Archive in Gillingham in Kent, there is an oil portrait, painted in 1795 'artist unknown', of a Captain Fiddes. The Museum acquired the portrait at auction in 1993, but has no further information on its provenance. The date is consistent with 'our' Captain Fiddes; the reader can decide on the validity of Smith's description. This

The 1795 portrait is reproduced by permission of the Royal Engineers Museum, Library & Archives. The back of the canvas is inscribed 'Captain Fiddes'.

was enough to convince me that not only was the story of the fort clear but also there was the added bonus that Captain Fiddes emerged from the historical shadows. As further confirmation, in 2015 a photograph, taken about 1970, of the portrait from Troup House appeared. It is the same man.

A photograph of the portrait seen at Troup House. It appears to be the same picture shown on the previous page from the Royal Engineers Museum.

The conclusion of this particular story is that Francis Garden of Troup died in 1804. All momentum for the use of Fort Fiddes for the purpose for which it was designed and built ended with the death of the driving force behind the project. The outline of the rampart is the only tangible reminder of its existence. As the last significant construction on the headland this is a suitable point to end the story.

10. FINAL THOUGHTS

Reflecting on the time spent and outcomes of this research prompts two sets of thoughts – the first relating to the nature of research, and the second concerned with Cullykhan and the questions posed at the outset.

Over the years, a number of people have said that the end of the research is never reached. I understand now what they meant. Researching can be wonderfully satisfying and exciting, especially when the missing bits of the story fall into place, but there can be as much pleasure when a small detail is confirmed. However it can be frustrating when sources do not agree on key facts. This has been true on many occasions from this research; as is clear from the text, it has not always been possible to resolve the differences.

Other frustrations include the sometimes voluminous, and overwhelmingly irrelevant, results that have to be sifted from entering 'Keith' (say) in a search engine online, or the complete absence of information where there had been grounds for optimism on the outcome. However, it is by means of these cyclical activities that views are formed and amended, arguments developed and, occasionally, the fog of history clears a little, although it has to be said that the fog in Scottish medieval history can be quite dense at times.

Contrasting activities may illustrate the potential pleasures of research. Despite a number of earlier attempts, usually thwarted by the weather, it took until early summer 2015 before, with friends, we managed to see Cullykhan and surrounding area, from the sea. The way in which this helped to crystallize ideas about the landscape and, in particular, the orientation of the headland was breathtaking. It was an essential complement to the many hours exploring the cliffs, studying the maps and taking photographs. Anyone interested in coastal sites will benefit from viewing the location from the sea at an early stage; you may well be replicating the experience of previous visitors and inhabitants.

Another example is the resolution of the story of Fort Fiddes. The sense of resolving a problem - long despaired of - was enhanced enormously when, having told Ed Knipe about my progress, he sent, by return, his recent discovery of the Journal which confirmed my work but also provided details of Captain Fiddes. Thus one question, which I had not really set out to answer at the outset, was settled.

Inevitably there remain unresolved questions. Where is the 'chapel of Trub'? What is under the ground at Findon? What did the castle look like at its best? How did people survive some of the harsh conditions there? Questions like these may never be answered with the information available now. Perhaps someone reading this will make a connection that has not been seen thus far. For some questions there is a need for more detailed combined archaeological and historical research.

Looking back to the questions posed in the Introduction it is fair to conclude that this account is only a small part of the whole story of those who lived, worked, and died on Cullykhan over centuries. For some periods enough has been found to establish an account. However, there are long gaps where insufficient evidence exists to formulate a story that can bring people to life.

The limited knowledge of the context of the first building on the site in the historic period – the house on the Knoll, if indeed it is a 'house' in a modern understanding of the term – is somehow emblematic of our knowledge of the site as a whole. It is speculation to ascribe its construction to a particular individual or family. There may be continuity of occupation from this part of the site to the castle site. Currently, the historical or archaeological evidence does not exist to resolve these issues. On the other hand, that allows the reader, and author alike, to frame a story to fit the limited known facts.

The castle was probably initially built around 1300 and abandoned in the early part of the seventeenth century. Occupation may not have been continuous but gap periods, if any, seem unlikely to have been long. Some significant events in the Wars of Independence undoubtedly impacted on those who lived there but then, as now, Troup was not a major population centre or place of great historical significance. The final phase of construction of the castle surely produced a fine building, reflecting perhaps the greater status and wealth of the Keith family; it would have dominated the immediate area. Its destruction and collapse, almost certainly initiated by substantial cliff erosion, have deprived us of the opportunity, for example, to see the full extent of the beautiful cobbled courtyard, and to understand better how the various people mentioned in this story lived.

Trying to explain Troup and some of its inhabitants leads inevitably to the conclusion that, like much of Scotland's past in the period in question, times were unsettled. The historical records are patchy and the archaeological evidence is not extensive enough to achieve any significant understanding of what their daily lives were like, what they thought and what they experienced.

Writing this in the dark depths of a Scottish winter it seems almost trite to say that life would not have been easy. Too often, conflict and violence never seemed far away. Ensuring adequate food supplies was likely to have been a continuing challenge made more difficult by uncertain weather, bad storms and outbreaks of plague. And yet for generations, people survived, and perhaps at times thrived there, enjoying the richness of a beautiful natural environment.

For these folk, Cullykhan may have been a special place; for some people it still is.

11. ADDENDUM

Undertaking historical research was a new experience for me. I have learned a lot, only some of which appears in this book. For someone brought up in Banffshire, I was aware from an early stage that there would be many distractions; seeing a reference to Cullen or Portsoy in an index was usually too difficult to resist. On the other hand, at the outset, there was, for example, no thought that place names would feature, to mention but one unexpected, but productive, digression.

Another dimension to such 'distractions' comes into play when others hear of what you are doing and share some story or information about Troup or the wider area. Contained here are examples of information, unknown to me at the beginning of my researches, that may be of interest to anyone who knows the area. I could not see how to integrate them into the story of Troup I was writing but did not want them to be lost. Almost by definition they are unconnected to each other.

Robert Petrie

Many people will have recordings of Scots Fiddle music; some, like us, will have a composition by Robert Petrie. Enthusiasts will no doubt know of him. Why is he mentioned here? Among his compositions are Robert Petrie's Lament for the Late Mr Garden of Troup, Miss Garden of Troup's strathspey, Mr Garden of Troup's Farewell to France, and Collie Can or Hells Lum (a reel). All told, there are at least 17 compositions with Troup allusions dating to the 1790s and early 1800s.

Collie Can or Hells Lum — a Reel by R. Petrie

Robert Petrie worked at Troup as a gamekeeper, a fact confirmed in public notices of Game Certificates, under Deputations. Examples appeared in the *Aberdeen Journal* newspaper of 24 November 1802 (where in the same notice there is mention of Francis Garden of Troup, who initiated the Fort Fiddes building project). Both men are similarly mentioned in the Journal of 11 November 1795. Robert Petrie is mentioned, too, in the Aberdeen Journal of August 1809.

Further detail on Robert Petrie and his music can be found in *The Scots Fiddle: Tunes, Tales & Traditions* by J Murray Neil (1991). There it states that Robert Petrie was born in Kirkmichael in Perthshire in 1767. *'He was regarded as an excellent fiddler … and also a noted composer.'* He was reputed to be a *'non – conformist'* and *'rather wild and unpredictable'*. It should be noted that there is a Kirkmichael in Banffshire.

Robert Petrie also features in the Presidential Address given by Dr. Grant to the Banffshire Field Club in December 1921; his informative paper *Strathspeys and Reels, Banffshire Composers* is published in the Transactions of the Society. In addition to some biographical information and details of publications of Petrie's four *Collections of Compositions*, it also tells us that *"For a number of years he was leader of The Laird of Troup's Band."*

The Black Milestone

The *Black Milestone* is a work of fiction set mainly in the Troup area at the beginning of World War II. The author, Catherine Gavin, wrote a number of historical works often with a French connection. The edition seen by the author was published in 1941 in London; Aberdeenshire Libraries has a copy.

Catherine Gavin's mother, to whom the book is dedicated, was a native of Troup. Places in the text will be familiar to anyone who knows the area. Some of the dialogue captures well the tenor and lilt of the Gamrie area.

The Northfield Murder Mystery

At the first presentation I did on my research I was asked if I knew about the murder, and subsequent court case, at Northfield. I had heard of neither. It took place in November 1756, and the victim was Alexander Keith, laird of Northfield. (This date does not tally exactly with the information contained in Appendix 2, but it is close.)

One source which describes the events is The Northfield Mystery, chapter 29 of *Classic Scottish Murder Stories* by Molly Whittington-Egan, published in Glasgow in 2007.

Alexander Garden's Paper

This paper *An Account of the Northside of the Coast of Buchan* was written in May 1683 by Alexander Garden of Troup. It can be found in Macfarlane's Geographical Collections. It is a description of the natural environment, with particular emphasis on seabirds, shellfish, crabs and fish, which were prevalent along the coast, and used for food, at that time. He also describes some features of the geology, including soils. The paper, which nowadays would probably be called a description of the ecology of the district, is a very interesting complement, from an earlier period, to the material in the Statistical Accounts.

The Fire at Frendraught

The name Frendraught features in the story of Troup through the activities of Duncan de Frendraught, but the fire in question belongs to a later period. The lands of Frendraught lie in the parish of Forgue about 7 miles north-east of Huntly.

The fire occurred on the night of 8/9 October 1630. Two members of the Gordon family, both called John, were among those who died in the fire in the tower of Frendraught Castle. One was laird of Rothiemay; the other was his kinsman, viscount Melgum, 5th son of George Gordon, 1st marquis of Huntly, the head of the Gordon family. The circumstances of these events, not unnaturally, proved contentious; indeed it proved to be the beginning of a bitter feud between the Gordons and the Crichtons.

Further information can be found in *Fire & Sword: the Gordon-Crichton Feud 1630-36* in *History Scotland, Nov/Dec 2009*. The article contains illustrations of the old castle, and its replacement built in 1656. A further source is the Proceedings of the Society of Antiquaries of Scotland (PSAS), volume 51 (1917) where in a paper headed *Note on some Stone Circles in Central Aberdeenshire* by James Ritchie there is mention of Frendraught (pages 30/1).

A New Fishing Station

Mr Garden Campbell of Troup proposes to establish a fishing town on the shore of Culican Bay, situated between Gardenston and Pennan, having convenient landing for Boats, and very near the fishing ground, with a spot highly commodious for Houses and Gardens. The Proprietor will give every encouragement towards the building of Houses etc. Application may be made immediately at Troup House, in person, or by letter, addressed by Banff.

(From Aberdeen Journal, 22 January 1817, page 1)

I am grateful to Douglas Lockhart for providing this reference originally published in *Scottish History No 88* (Spring 2014). In a period when many landowners sought to establish new villages, this refers to a planned settlement which did not materialise.

APPENDIX 1

THE LANDS OF TROUP

Introduction

The purpose here is to set down some information about the lands of Troup and surrounding areas. My initial aim was to identify boundaries for the lands of Troup, and key places within it such as Lethnot and Northfield, for as much of the period of occupation on Cullykhan as possible. As ownership and definition of landholdings has clearly been significant in Scotland throughout recorded history - if not earlier – the hope was that this would be feasible. The fleeting desire, early in the research, to produce maps illustrating the changes to boundaries at times of significant events soon assumed the status of a task that could be advanced only if sources were found where this was already clear. The necessary resources have not been found.

The sources which were found are varied in nature and, inevitably, the information is incomplete. A greater level of detail is usually helpful, but not always. For example, places mentioned in the definition of boundaries in legal cases may no longer be readily identifiable. More generally, it is usually not possible to be precise about the length of time any boundary or feature described was maintained.

Sometimes it is reasonable to conjecture that the boundary being described is a long lasting one; for example, the boundary between Troup and Aberdour in the Tore of Troup. However, when only the names of lands and farms are given without further detail, great care is required in drawing conclusions. Such difficulties are not reduced when the sources are citing descriptions or events many years apart. Although later plans and maps, and other written sources, are always interesting and sometimes very useful, the temptation to extrapolate backwards in time must be resisted.

The edited map opposite may help the reader make sense of this part of Buchan. For the sake of clarity, Cullykhan is not named, a line drawn from Northfield through Troup House goes to the headland where the excavations took place.

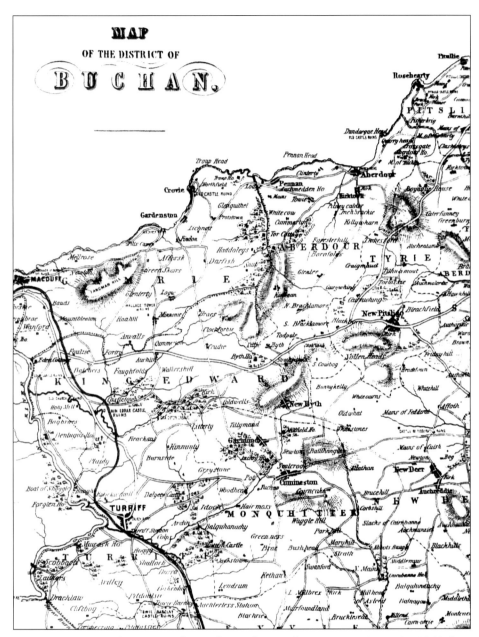

Part of the map from Pratt's Buchan, dating from approximately 1858 (see Bibliography). It shows the boundary of Gamrie parish heading south in the Tore of Troup (Tor Cottage is marked) before heading WSW south of Minnonie and Mountbletton to the River Deveron. No single map found includes all the places in Troup in this Appendix. The map shown in 'Earliest Historic References' on page 45 can also be of assistance in this Appendix.

Boundaries of Troup

Some parts of the boundary appear to be clear. The eastern boundary of Troup, which, at different times, was the western boundary of the lands of Auchmedden, or the barony of Aberdour, or the earldom of Buchan, is of Troup running south from the coast at Nethermill along the burn in the Tore. This was also the boundary between historic Banffshire and Aberdeenshire; in fact, it is only in recent times that the burn has ceased to be an important secular or administrative boundary, though it remains part of the boundary of the parish of Gamrie.

In medieval times, Troup and Glendowachy were bounded to the south, and partially to the east, by the lands of Kingedward. In the Comyn period, and probably for some time before, Kingedward was a sizeable proportion of the earldom of Buchan. Some idea of the boundary may be gleaned from the names of places quoted on relevant charters. Included in Kingedward, for example, are Scatterty, Byth, Fisherie, Blackton, Montcoffer and Eden in the lower Deveron. Eastwards Glencuthil, Auchmedden and Tyrie were also included. Fortrie to the south is also in Kingedward. Similarly, Findon, Logie, Crovie and Northfield, to name a few, feature in Troup.

The names of lands known to be in Glendowachy (or Doune) and Troup give a close, and convincing, match between the boundary and extent of the parish of Gamrie and the combined area of Glendowachy and Troup. Indeed, the initial definition of these land areas may have happened about the same time.

The next task was to identify the boundary between Glendowachy and Troup within the parish of Gamrie. No source has been found which specifies this in detail, but there are pointers giving possible clues.

In the petition of 1304 submitted by Hamelin de Trop, he complains that the lands of Troup, specifically Findon and Logie were burnt and harried by Sir Duncan de Frendraught and Sir Ranald le Chen. Bannerman, in his book on Glendowachy, concludes from the terms of this petition that the boundary between Glendowachy and Troup had Findon and Logie on the east side with Minnonie and Draidland to the west (Bannerman, 1879, 12).

The likelihood is that St John's Kirk on Mhor Head was the main place of worship in Glendowachy, from the eleventh century onwards. Bearing in mind too that the original grant to the Abbey of Arbroath also mentions a 'chapel at Troup' (as yet unidentified), the eastern boundary of Glendowachy must be to the east of St John's Kirk. This would mean the lands of Melrose and Cullen to the west were in Glendowachy.

Often places of worship were established close to boundaries. If that is the case here, a potential, and arguably the obvious, boundary is likely to be the Den of Afforsk, a distinctive feature in the landscape.

This view looks south along the Den of Minnonie in what could be called the extension of the Den of Afforsk. The break of slope is less steep than in the Den of Afforsk but it is a clear feature in the landscape. Drainage is a continuing concern here. At the southern end of the Den, the remains of Ha'Hill Castle are (just) visible in the centre of the picture.

Following the natural line of Afforsk south from the sea to the southern boundary of the parish, Cushnie and Minnonie would be in Troup with Draidland and Pitgair being in Glendowachy. The southern part of the boundary would follow the Burn of Minnonie. As an aside, this area is one of the few which received detailed comment in the Statistical Account of 1845 for Gamrie parish.

A further noteworthy feature is that the unmistakable profile of Bennachie is visible from the southern end of this proposed boundary. A route beginning at the northern end of the Den of Afforsk with a distinctive landmark visible from the southern end of the Den of Minnonie is one that can be easily described. Its potential as an important feature in historic times is evident.

Three points require further comment. First, it is clear that the course of the Burn of Minnonie has been subject to change occasioned by the development of mills and possible land improvement measures. The precise extent of this is not known.

The second point concerns the position of the ruins of Ha'Hill Castle. The boundary between Troup and Glendowachy proposed above lies to the east of the ruins. Without a major change in the course of the Burn of Minnonie, that places Ha'Hill in Glendowachy. Also potentially relevant are the terms of the charter of 1413 that mentions Hayninghill (taken to be Ha'Hill) in the context of the barony of Troup. This difficulty may be explained when it is recalled that this charter was produced when branches of the earl Marischal's family had control of both Glendowachy and Troup. As it was the earl Marischal himself who was reserving Ha'Hill – together with two other mottes in Troup – and the three locations are likely to have been traditional centres (perhaps for the local administration of justice), this may be enough to explain the position. As mentioned in the main text, this was a time when adjustments to landholdings were being made within the wider Keith family.

Undoubtedly, from the early fifteenth century onwards, significant, and sometimes frequent, change happened to lands within Gamrie. The boundary proposed above may have lasted about 100 years before pressures to ensure land was available for the burgeoning number of Keiths obliged the earl Marischal to make further adjustments.

The third point is that some changes in the western boundary of Troup appear to have been made at a later date. The plan of 1767, a portion of which is included below, has Minnonie and Avaulds in Troup. To discover when this happened and for how long, requires further research.

There are later references which show that changes took place. For example, in relation to Glendowachy, in 1528 John, earl of Buchan, obtained a charter. According to Bannerman, 'this marks the summit of the prosperity in the affairs of Glendowachie'. The details are as follows.

At Stirling, 12th August, the King confirmed to John, Earl of Buchan, and his heirs … the lands and barony of Glendowachy, alias Downe, viz the lordship lands of Downe with the mill, fishing and smithy; the lands of Mailros, with the outset, mill and fishing; Fortre, with the mill and the outset; … the Castle of Banff with the castlehill and orchards; the offices of sheriff and coroner in the County of Banff; the lands of Petgar with the mill; Mynone and Cartrilzeade [a clerical error for Dradeleane]; Culane in the county of Banff; the lands of Achmedden, with the fishing, … (Bannerman, 1897, 24).

A later example in the National Archives provides a description of the lands of Troup in 1792.

the lands and barony of Troup with two mills and mill lands thereof, the lands of Middletown, Logie, Snab, Reidoups, Poweston, excepting the lands of Northfield and the part called Twicketfield and others which were erected in the barony of Troup, the lands of Cushnie, Wester and Easter Findon, Fairniebrae, Crovie, Protstown and Protstoun Stenwell, Auquhorsk, Pitgair and mill and mill lands thereof, Avaulds Castle and Castlehill of Pitgair, Lichnet, Minonie, Old and New Dreaidlands, Whitehill, Greenscairs all in parish of Gamry and sheriffdom of Banff… (dated 7/5/1792) (NAS, GD/57/237).

In these two examples, the boundary between Troup and Glendowachy (or Doune) moved as Pitgair and Minnonie, for example, appear in both charters. Other charters would also show show differing configurations of landholdings at different times.

Lands within Troup

In the period under consideration, two significant areas have been mentioned in the text, Lethnot and Northfield.

Lethnot

The original grant of Lethnot by Robert Corbet to Kinloss Abbey was described earlier. The evidence suggests that Lethnot remained a defined entity under Kinloss Abbey up to the later sixteenth century, the time of the Reformation. The original charter has not been found, but in the court case mentioned below, Robert, the then Abbot of Kinloss Abbey, produced a charter of 1319 from which the details of the march are quoted.

By 1518 Patrick Cheyne of Esslemont was the vassal of the Abbot of Kinloss in the lands of Lethnot.

In 1537 there was a court case between Patrick Cheyne of Essilmonth, feuar and proprietor of the lands of Lethnot, and his superior, Robert, abbot of Kinloss, on the one hand and Gilbert Keith of Troup and his superior, lord William, earl Marischal, disputing the march between Lethnot and Troup. As part of the judgement, which was in favour of Patrick Cheyne, the description of the march is as follows.

> *.... frae the Lang Furd, the midmest furd of the the three fordis ascendand up the Hill of Findon and to northt syde of the same on to the Cairnslaw callit Clochtyne alias Teorieclamchyne and fraethin west to the highgate to the heid of Pollisdone and in commonty frae the said gate to the heid of Pollisdone, ascendand up the Hill of Findon on to the law upon the heicht of the same wher ther sal be put ane stain cross and fraethin descendand down to the brek of the moss callit the Crosslacks as it is pairtit and merchit be the saidis parties / swa that it sal be leisum to the said Gilbert and his ayris to labour and manur be west the said merchis of Crosslacks and Todlaw with cornis or ony vthirways. And it sal not be leisum to the said Gilbert to labour nor manur the common mure liand betwixt the Halkden and the Todlaw... (Spalding Club, 1847, 366-7).*

This picture, taken from the track between Northfield and Crovie, shows part of Lethnot. Crovie is off to the right of this image. Although an old castle is marked on some maps and plans, its current location has not been identified on the ground.

Patrick Cheyne was granted permanent possession of Lethnot in 1559. He later enhanced his holdings in 1571 by taking possession of the barony of Aberdour (see below), but in 1577, he was again in dispute with a Keith of Troup. These local examples illustrate the nature and frequency of disagreements over land issues at that time.

Northfield

Northfield became a separate defined entity in 1462 when John Keith received a new charter for the ten merk lands of Northfield (NAS,GO36/308). These lands remained in the Keith family, the branch known as Keiths of Northfield, for many generations (see Appendix 2). Like Lethnot they appear unchanged during this period.

They are described in the following extract dated 1760, which was difficult to decipher

> *… lands of Northfield lying between the house and Inclosures of Troup and the sea as the same is bounded by the Sea on the north until the burn of Northfield or Culycan run into the sea at the east point of the said lands thereby --- poned(?) and by the said burn in the south and by the remainder of the said lands of Northfield on the west by the following march. Viz. Beginning at the said burn of Northfield a little above the west dykes of the Halins(?) Inclosures of Troup and descending by Cairns and spadeholes lately made to the top of the Brae and from thence turning towards the sea and going from cairn to cairn as the same were then sell to the sea with the multures of the said lands thereby …*

> *But reserving the road through the said to the Miln of Cullycan, as also reserving the same privilege of the Kilty wrecks upon the Sea Banks of the said lands (NAS, GD57/182).*

The 1767 plan (MS 2626 in the Archives of the University of Aberdeen) clearly shows the boundaries of Northfield. Bearing in mind that detail of the coastline within the lands of Northfield is not drawn accurately. In other words, you look in vain for the detail of Troup Head, although Cullykhan is there.

The following extracts are included to add more detail with respect to some lands near Troup. This small sample is indicative of the extent of the changes made and, on occasions, the detail available. They may serve as starting points for those who wish to pursue research further.

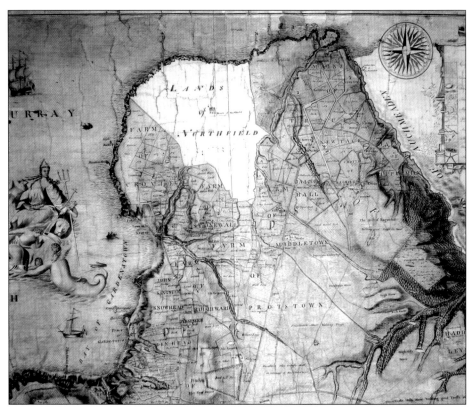

This is a small part of a plan of the lands of Troup prepared by the well-known surveyor John Home in 1767 and now in the Archives of the University of Aberdeen. It shows the delineation of the lands of Northfield, when Northfield became a separate estate in 1462. Note that where, in all other plans, you would see the farm of Lichnot, here it is called the Farm of Roughward. By the time a later plan was prepared in the nineteenth century, Lichnot has reappeared as the name of the farm (DD21/1/47 in Aberdeenshire Archives). It is also worth remembering the quotation where "Lichnet' is mentioned as part of the lands of Troup, in a bond in the National Archives dated May 1792.

The Boundary between Cullen and Melrose

William Bannerman had access to papers associated with a court hearing in 1618 in which the Barclays of Tollie were involved. The text here includes portions which appear to be from original papers together with additional comments, mostly in brackets, by William Bannerman. It shows how boundaries were described, and the ease with which differences of interpretation might arise.

Beginning at the Auld Haven of Cullen and the mouth of the Burn of Melrose following upwards along the course of that burn to the mill ford or kirk ford (doubtless now the site of the bridge at the Mill of Melrose) and so by the back of the mills at Cullen (the waulk mill and meal mill before mentioned) to where the burn of Clachden enters the burn of Melrose; then upwards by the course of the Claithburn to the head of the burn at "ane mekill grey stane" – perhaps the venerable clach or stone whence the den takes its name. Hence the boundary follows a series of potholes in the moss, where we encounter such names as the Black Myre or Blak Delffes, and passing seemingly by the eastern end of the hamlet of Langman Hill, then non-existent, it touches the northern end of the Moss of Montbletton; thence it follows the White Stripe downwards to the Bauds of Cullen enclosing within its reaches the Fluiket Burn (seemingly the head of the burn of Myrehouse) and returning by certain pot holes through mosses it passes through the Seatown bog and again reaches the sea called the Fluikett Loch, to the west of the Auld Haven of Cullen (Bannerman, 1897, 7).

Lands of Aberdour

On 17th July 1571, William Lord Borthwick sold to Patrick Cheyne of Esslemont all the lands and Barony of Aberdour, namely the Manor Place and ecclesiastical mansion of Aberdour, Clintertie, Ardlayhill, Killequharn, and Pennand, Tyrie, Mekil Auchrie etc., as one whole and free Barony to be called in all future time the Barony of Aberdour (Ferguson, 1913, 263).

Killequharn, mentioned here and in the next extract, is not the same place as Cullykhan.

In 1660 Patrick Cheyne sold to Master John Cheyne of Pitfichie inter alia the Mains of Aberdour with the corn mill and Killiequharne with the ports etc., and in the same year with his consent sold to Patrick Cheyne, his lawful son by Magdalen Fraser his wife, the Manor Place or Manis of Aberdour with the tower and fortalice of Dundarg, Ardlahill, Killiequharne, Clentertie, Badiscoller, Greindyk, Pennand, and its quarry with the mill of Aberdour etc., in the Barony and Parish of Aberdour. In 1605 a charter of appreciation of these lands belonging to Patrick Cheyne of Esslemont was

granted to Alexander Fraser Apparent of Philorth. In 1608 Fraser
sold the lands of Tippertie and Scattertie, the Mayns of Aberdour
with the Manor of Dundarg, Pennan, Killiequharne, Clintertie and
Ardlahill to Andrew son of John Fraser of Quarrelbus. In 1624
Andrew passed the Aberdour lands on to John, eldest son of the
deceased Sir Alexander Fraser of Fraserburgh, and in 1630
Alexander Fraser Younger of Philorth granted Aberdour, the tower
and fortalice of Dundarg, Kilquharne, Ardlayhill, Clintertie, and
Pennan to Lord Pitsligo, who, in 1635 granted Clintertie and
Pennan to George Baird of Auchmedden. In 1637 Alexander Lord
Forbes of Pitsligo was served heir of his father in the lands and
Barony of Aberdour (Ferguson, 1913, 263).

Lands of Glencuthil

In 1428 King James confirmed a charter of John, Earl of Buchan,
Constable of France, Chamberlain of Scotland, by which he gave to
Patrick of Ogilvy, Sheriff of Angus, and Christian of Keith, his
spouse, our dearest cousin, the whole Lordship of Glencuthil with
the pertinents, namely Echmedane and le Glenhoussis, Kynbene,
Bith, Petmakaldor, Towy, Bothmakaly, le Saltscotis, Inchebrek
(Ferguson, 1913, 247).

Conclusion

It needs to be stressed again that these snapshots illustrate the complexity of trying to gain a full understanding of what took place when. More research could clarify a number of points. However, the caveats about research of this topic in this geographical area mentioned at the beginning of the Appendix remain significant in limiting the extent of the conclusions that can be drawn.

Finally, the contrasting levels of detail seen in this limited selection of examples do illustrate that, against a background where ownership and definition of landholdings were matters of great importance in medieval Scotland, it is easier to understand how litigation and violence often had their roots in questions of title, inheritance and apportioning of land.

APPENDIX 2

NOTE of DESCENT of KEITHS of NORTHFIELD
FROM the MARISCHALL FAMILY

(This information comes from a submission by the last-named George Keith of Northfield to his solicitors as part of an attempt to establish his lawful descent from the Keith earl Marischals and Keiths of Troup. The original is in the National Archives of Scotland GO 36/308.)

John de Keth got from his father Sir Robert the Great Marischall the Barrony of Troup by Charter Confirmation under the Great Seal in 1413 which in 1462 he resigns and got from his nephew William second earl Marischall a Charter of the Ten Merk Lands of the said Barrony called Northfield. He married first Eupham Daughter of King Robert II by Eupham Daughter of Hugh Earl of Ross and second Eliza Menzies Daughter of Menzies of Durrisdein(?).

James, his son, succeeded 1467; wife Margaret Fraser, daughter of Fraser of Doors.

John, his brother, succeeded 1483; wife Jean Abernethy, daughter of Saltown.

Archibald, his son, succeeded 1501; wife Isabel Skene, daughter of Skene.

John, his son, succeeded 1527; wife Janet Burnet, daughter of Leys.

William, his son, succeeded 1550; wife Violeta Cheyne, daughter of Auchmedden.

John, his son, succeeded 1578; wife Marjory Keith, daughter of Troup.

William, his son, succeeded 1603; wife Marjory Ogilvie, daughter of Boyne.

John, his son, succeeded 1628; wife Ann Baird, daughter of Auchmedden.

George, his son, succeeded 1640; wife Janet Gordon, daughter of Bismore.

Alexander, his son, succeeded 1689; wife Sophia Fraser, daughter of Memsie.

Alexander, his son, succeeded 1712; wife Margaret Gordon, daughter of Techmuiry.

George, his son, succeeded 1754; wife Eliza Whyt, daughter of Ardlayhill.

George, his son; wife Janet Dunlop, Cherry Valley, America

Note: The Northfield Murder Mystery concerns the death of Alexander Keith (succeeded 1712) and the subsequent court case. It is interesting to note that Alexander's second wife, Helen Watt a fisherman's daughter from Crovie and a key person in the 'mystery', is not mentioned in the above list.

APPENDIX 3

SOME PLACE NAMES IN TROUP

By Jennifer McKay

All references to old Scots usages are taken from the Concise Scots Dictionary.

Farms on Troup

The Gamrie section of Gordon of Straloch's 1654 map has no Scots names on it; they are all of Gaelic origin. However, Gordon does not name every farm and settlement. He ignores several Scots-English names, which, we know from charter evidence, pre-date his map. Among them are: Middleton, Protston, Stonewell, Jacobshall and Dubston. These are all holdings on the Lands of Troup. Clearly, the naming of Troup alone was sufficient for Gordon's purposes, whatever these were.

Middleton appears in 1559 as 'Myddiltoune' in Inquisicio Walter Berclay de Tolly. The element **ton** is an Old English word for 'farm'. In Scotland, **ton** is also rendered as 'tone', 'toun' or 'town'. 'An area of arable land on an estate, occupied by a number of farmers as co-tenants, in use from the late 14th century' (Concise Scots Dictionary) It is conceivable, then, that the name 'Myddiltoune' had been in use for a century and a half before it appeared on the 1559 document.

In 1488, the modern 'Protston' was spelled 'Pratistone'. James VI regranted 'Pratstoun' to the earl Marischal in 1592. The Register of the Great Seal of 1663 has 'Pratston'. By 1767 the estate map is using the spelling 'Protstown'. There is very little difference in the local pronunciation of the short [a] and the short [o] sounds and consequently these sounds are, at times, interchanged. The derivation of the name is possibly from the Latin **pratum,** meaning 'meadow' or 'meadow grass'. Another likely example of this Latin usage is the farm name of Pratis in the parish of Largo in the East Neuk of Fife.

Stonewell is first shown on the estate plan of 1767 as 'Stonewall', suggesting that the farm had stone walls or stone wall footings, rather than clay or turf, and perhaps implying it was the first on the estate to be so constructed. Estate inventories of the nineteenth century allude to clay built farm buildings. There are no stone dykes in the area; further suggesting that the name is a description of the farm building. The name had morphed into the modern 'Stonewell' by the time of the 1869 OS map.

I have found no evidence to help with the source of the name Jacobshall. It is possible that the farm is named for the biblical Jacob. There are several examples of biblical farm names in eastern Scotland: Jericho, Babylon, Gomorrah.

The name Dubston presumably harks back to the old Gaelic naming strategy of describing the landscape. **Dubs** is the Banffshire Scots for 'puddles'. Dubston sits by the road, which may have been waterlogged, and muddy at this point.

Laws

A glance at the map shows us a scattering of 'Laws': Melrose Law, Northfield Law, Collie Law, the Law and Law Hill. These names first appear on the 1869 map and without other written evidence we cannot say when the term 'Law' was adopted in Gamrie. The Concise Scots Dictionary's definition of **law** is:

(1) *a rounded or conical hill, frequently isolated or conspicuous, used from the late 14th century in place-names*

(2) *an artificial mound, specifically a grave-mound, used from the late 16th to early 19th centuries.*

Melrose Law is a Bronze Age burial cairn and not a hill at all. There is scant surface evidence of prehistoric burial monuments on the other abovementioned 'Laws' but neither are they conical hills. The First Edition OS map records 'An Urn found' on Northfield Law and 'Human Remains found' on the Law. The Rev. Wilson writing in the Old Statistical Account in the 1790s tells us that there are 'several tumuli' in the parish and he knew of one which had been excavated to reveal an urn and human bones.

In 1683, Alexander Garden of Troup, responding to a request for information about the area from Robert Sibbald, the Geographer Royal, who had been commissioned by Charles II to produce a geography of Scotland, wrote:

Betwixt the watermouth of Devern six miles westward of this, and the Church of Raithen nine miles eastwards of this, alongst the coast or at least within a mile or two of it, are severall verie great heaps of stones; the biggest of which is Cairnbo three miles westwards of this. It will be of perpendicular height from top to bottom twixt 29 and 30 foots English measure. Of these in the forsaid bounds there are seven or eight, besides severall other lesser mounts of earth and stone. The common tradition is that these were the sumptuous tombs of our ancestors, but it is somewhat odd so many of them in so little bounds.

The areas designated 'Law', although on high ground, are not hills and very likely the location of burial cairns. With the exception of Melrose Law, the cairns have more or less disappeared, probably to be used as building stone, road metal or cleared to make ploughing easier.

Dens

A striking feature of the Gamrie landscape are the 'dens', deep, narrow valleys created by the scouring action of glaciers along fault lines. Chambers' definition of the word **den** is 'a narrow valley, a dean (Scot)'. The Concise Scots dictionary adds that they usually have trees and that the term has been in use since the sixteenth century. There are dens throughout eastern Scotland.

A typical den in Gamrie parish; looking south along the Den of Afforsk.

Close to Troup there are several: Den of Afforsk, Den of Findon, Powie's Den, Braco Den, Protston Den, Crovie Den etc. Groome's Gazetteer (1882) describes them thus:

> *Several mighty chasms cleave the rampart (ie the coastal cliffs) from top to bottom, and look like stupendous rents made by shock of earthquake; they yawn widely at the shore, and take the form of dells towards the interior; and they have zig-zag projections, with protuberances on one side corresponding to depressions or hollows on the other. The most easterly of these is at Cullykhan, near Troup House...*

By far the biggest and most spectacular of these dens is the Tore of Troup. Pont calls it 'Glens of Trowip', which may imply that the term **den** had not yet reached Gamrie at the end of the sixteenth century. **Tore** is a form of the verb 'to tear' and the word conveys the perception that the land has been ripped apart, as described in the gazetteer.

Coastal Features

Names of coastal features barely register on the early maps. The first map of the area, surveyed by Pont in the 1590s does not name Cullykhan, although he includes 'Ghemmry head' and 'Trowip head'. While Gordon of Straloch depicts 'Trowp', it appears to be the old castle on the Cullykhan peninsula that he has marked on his map. The Troup estate papers and the estate plan of 1767 refer to the coast in the vaguest of terms. 'Kitty Viack Rocks' are indicated on the estate plan as the shore between Downie Bay and Lion's Head. That is the sum and substance of coastal information provided. It is not

The 'Kitty Viack Rocks' (1767), now called The Coves.

clear if 'Kitty Viack Rocks' is a name or simply a note on the plan that this is the section of coast where kittiwakes are found.

These 'Kitty Viack Rocks' of 1767 merit further mention. It appears from a charter of confirmation of 1807 from Northfield to Francis Garden of Troup that, 'the same privileges of the 'Kittyweaks' up the sea rocks' are reconfirmed.

The Old Statistical Account notes that:

Some people are fond of eating the Kitty's; but the shooting of them is a favourite diversion every year. The season for this is usually the last week in July.

In 1835 there was concern that kittiwake numbers were in decline as a consequence of poaching and the theft of eggs. At that time kittiwakes were commercially exploited for their feathers to the financial benefit of the landowner. Notices were to be posted in churches and elsewhere to remind parishioners of the ban on taking birds and eggs.

The 1869 OS map is the first to provide names of coastal features. There are forty-eight named rocks, reefs, beaches and headlands from More Head to Cullykhan, on this map. Subsequent editions show far fewer.

Immediately below More Head lies a wave cut rock platform called 'Licks of Crackie'. 'Lick' is an anglicisation of the Gaelic **leac** meaning a 'slab of stone' or a 'flag stone'. Another version of **leac** is found offshore just east of Pennan Head at 'Drostan's Leak'. 'Crackie' remains a mystery.

'The Gammels', 'a group of rocks detached from the shore a short distance, on the west side of Gamrie Bay' (OS Name Book) are depicted just off More Head. The name was confirmed to the Ordnance Survey by William Nicol, fisher Gardenstown and John Watt, pilot, Gardenstown. **Gammels** was an old Scots word for 'twins'.

Between The Gammels and Gardenstown is a group of rocks called 'Pecking Craig'. The word 'craig' derives from the Gaelic **creag**, a 'rock' and is used extensively along the Gamrie coast. 'Craig' is a loan word from Gaelic. That is, a word, which has been adopted into a different language, sometimes with a slightly different spelling, and continues to be used, as it would have been in its original language. English has absorbed many loan-words, for example, the French 'gateau', the Italian 'spaghetti', the

German 'sauerkraut' and so on. Such words are usually borrowed because the adopting language does not have its own word for the object or phenomenon.

The 'Muckle Wife' rock

The next mentioned rock is the 'Muckle Wife', in more modern English, 'Big Woman', with **muckle** meaning 'big' coming into use from the late seventeenth century. The 'Muckle Wife' is described in the Name Book as 'A large rock, standing erect on the foreshore near Gardenstown'.

Close to the 'Muckle Wife' on the first edition OS map is 'St John's Stone':

A large boulder on the shore near Gardenstown; the origin of the tradition connected with the name has been lost.

I would venture to suggest that the boulder was deemed, at one time, to have been a player in the legend of the Battle of the Bleedy Pots. In the year 1004, so the story goes, a raiding party of "Danes" camped on the level ground near the church of St John. The Mormaer of Buchan, determined to dislodge them, prayed to St John the Evangelist for assistance. Then with his fighting men he climbed the slope above the camp under cover of darkness and threw stones and rolled boulders down on the unsuspecting Danes who were put to flight, some jumping over the cliff, to their deaths, in a futile effort to escape. St John must surely have answered the Mormaer's prayers and this rock may have entered folk memory as a boulder from the battle.

Looking from the western side of Findon, the view emphasizes the steepness of the slope on which the battle with the Danes was fought in 1004. On the shore below are the remnants of later rock falls with the Muckle Wife rock prominent.

My search for this boulder has drawn a blank. The Gamrie folk I have asked have never heard of 'St John's Stone'. It may be that the boulder was destroyed in 1913 when stone was being quarried at the end of the point for use in the Gardenstown harbour improvements.

Closer to Gardenstown, just where the sandy beach meets the rocky foreshore, directly below the church, is 'St John's Well', a spring which may have a mythical connection with St John. The Name Book informants were: Mr Kennedy of Gardenstown, Mr Fordyce, merchant of Gardenstown and Mr Watson of Knowhead. The entry reads:

A fine spring of fresh water covered at high Tides, situated beneath St John's Kirk, this well was held sacred by the former inhabitants.

Not far from the harbour entrance at Gardenstown is a long reef called Craigandargity, described in the Name Book as:

a large mass of conglomerate rock Surrounded by the sea at flood tides; Situated in Gamrie Bay, opposite the village of Gardenstown.

Taken from above the harbour at Gardenstown at low tide, the extent of the reef called Craigandargity is clear. At high tide, much less is apparent to any mariner.

Here we have another instance of 'craig' but what about the 'andargity'? The element **an** derives from the Gaelic 'of the', so it is the rock of the 'dargity'. **Darg** is Scots for 'young whiting' and the **ity** is a diminutive suffix suggesting small whitings. There is another old Scots word **dargie** meaning 'the fry of the coalfish' which might also fit the bill. We can turn again to Garden of Troup's letter of 1683 for further comment:

Whitings and Flooks are most common with us in the summertime. The small fishes are found within a mile of the shoar, but the great fishes at a greater distance.

Craigandargity is close to the shore. So it seems its meaning may indeed be the 'rock of the small whitings or coalfish'.

Offshore, between Gardenstown and Crovie are 'The Powies'. Scots **pow** is the head of a human being or an animal, the crown of the head, the scalp (late fifteenth century, Concise Scots Dictionary). These rocks have also been named on the map as 'Powie Bushes'. 'Bushes' is seaweed, attached to rocks, (John O'Neill, pers. comm.) which moves with the current, giving an impression of hair on a head.

A rocky point on the shore between Gardenstown and Crovie is called the 'Sneuk' or the 'Snook'. There is an old Scots verb to **snoke** meaning to sniff, which suggests that the point of rock has been judged to have nose-like attributes.

'Dark Dungeon' as recorded in the Name Book is:

a large natural cavern, in the Cliff at Crovie Head.

This name was perhaps a fairly new at the time of the First Edition as it is completely English but it is a name, I believe, now unknown to local Gamrie folk. It is one of the names, which does not appear on the modern map.

Nearby are 'Maw Craigs'. **Maw** is a late nineteenth century Scots word for 'sea gull', used particularly in Orkney and Shetland. Gamrie has close associations with Shetland through the fishing and it is logical to suppose that Shetland usages have entered the Gamrie vocabulary.

Collie Head is at the eastern end of Gamrie Bay; the name may derive from the Gaelic, **coille**, a 'wood'.

Three fingers of rock extend into the sea at the foot of Troup Head. Thirlet Point is the westerly finger. **Thirlet** is the past participle of the verb to **thirl**. **Thirl** has several meanings, one of which is 'to perforate' or 'to bore through'. It is, therefore, a point through which the sea has eroded a gap. Nether Stair, to the east, is a very apt description as these rock slabs descend like steps, towards the Ladder Creek. **Nether** appeared in the Scots language with the meaning of 'lower' in the fourteenth century but, of course, could have been applied to this rock formation at any time from then onwards. Adjacent to the Nether Stair is the Hare's Nose. Seen from a certain angle from the sea, a likeness to a hare's head is discernible.

Two names on the map contain personal name elements; they are Cowper's Craig and Booth's Clock and both contain hints of Gaelic. 'Craig' has already been explained. 'Clock' is likely to be an anglicised version of the Gaelic **clach** or 'cloch' meaning a 'stone'.

The stretch of coast which runs eastwards from Downie Bay to Lion's Head is called simply The Coves, a word which was, from the late fifteenth century to the early seventeenth century, a Scots term for 'caves'. These cliffs, which are riddled with caves, correspond to the 'Ketty Viack Rocks' of the 1767 estate plan. A feature here is The Bell House, a high cave at the foot of the cliff in the shape of a medieval church hand bell.

The next named promontory is Lion's Head. Your writer is yet to be convinced that it resembles a lion. It is a modern English name and, as such, along with Dark Dungeon, Castle Point and The Bell House, is somewhat anomalous, as most of the names hereabouts have Scots and/or Gaelic components. Lion's Head is home to Hell's Lum, a spectacular blowhole and an example of Scots usage, **lum** being Scots for 'chimney'. During northerly gales spray rises from Hell's Lum like smoke, hence the name, according to Rev Wilson, the author of the Old Statistical Account. Rev Wilson's comments are the basis for subsequent descriptions in nineteenth century gazetteers and other writing of the period.

Between Lion's Head and Cullykhan/Castle Point is a dogleg sea channel through the rocks called The Pot. The Name Book records:

> a small deep creek on the coast Situated between the Lion's Head and the Devil's Dining Room.

The Concise Scots Dictionary has it that from the late fourteenth to early in the seventeenth century the word **pot** meant a 'deep chasm or abyss of hell.' The Pot is situated around 100 metres from Hell's Lum to its south and about 100 metres from the Devil's Dining Room to the east. This close concentration of a group of names with nether-worldly associations begs the questions of why and why here. One wonders if satanic practices were ever performed in this very secluded spot.

The Devil's Dining Room, also locally known as the 'Deil's Kitchen', is a cave on the north side of Cullykhan headland, extravagantly described in the nineteenth century geographical gazetteers, in words plagiarised from the Old Statistical Account:

This view is taken from the headland at Cullykhan, with Lion's Head dominating. To the left, Hell's Lum is visible, but the main feature in the centre is the Pot, a channel through the wave-cut platform. The fallen rocks, in the left foreground, indicate the entrance to the Devil's Dining Room.

> *Another subterranean passage, through a peninsula about 150 yards long from sea to sea, through which a man can with difficulty creep. At the north end of this narrow passage is a cave about 20 feet high, 30 broad and 150 long; containing not less than 90,000 cubic feet. The whole is supported by immense columns of rock, is exceedingly grand, and has a wonderfully fine effect, after a person has crept through the narrow passage. This place has got the name of the Needle's Eye.*

Mr Wilson does not mention the name Devil's Dining-room, nor does he name the peninsula. However, the artist John Claude Nattes, who produced an etching of the Devil's Dining Room in 1799 for his publication, Scotia Depicta, captions his drawing 'Troup Head' (sic). The description of the cave provided by Mr Wilson does not accord with its present dimensions. It is much smaller than he described. It seems likely that more than two centuries of coastal erosion have reduced the dimensions of the cave. There is ample evidence of major landslips and rock falls in and around the cave.

From the back of the cave a passage runs through the headland to an opening near Cullykhan beach which is marked on the modern map as the Needle's Eye, known locally as the 'Needle's E'e'. The castle sat immediately above this fracture in the headland on what is now Cullykhan's narrowest point.

The extensive rockfall in the foreground, adjacent to the entrance of the Devil's Dining Room, suggests roof collapse which would explain why the present day cave is smaller than the description given in the Old Statistical Account.

Currently, there is some confusion about the name of the headland. In 1767 it was referred to as 'Castle Hill'; in 1804 'Coulie Cann, or Castlehill'; in 1869 'Castle Point'; now it seems to be acquiring the name of 'Fort Fiddes', as evidenced by the signpost at the road end, and various internet entries. The name 'Fort Fiddes' was given by Garden of Troup, in 1804, only to the battery, in honour of Captain Fiddes who executed its design and construction. In 1869, a later Garden of Troup provided the Ordnance Survey with name 'Castle Point'. However, for the folk who live in Gamrie, it is Cullykhan.

Knowledge of names is being lost. Of the 48 names marked on the First Edition OS map, only 18 appear on the modern 1:25,000 map and while some of the missing 30 names are remembered within the local community, others have been forgotten.

On the other hand, knowledge, not captured on maps, has been retained. It is widely claimed that Garden of Troup founded Gardenstown in 1720 but this would appear to be a fallacy as parish baptismal records, which were kept from 1704, show that there was a village on the shore of Gamrie Bay called Powieston. This name has been lost to usage and replaced by Gardenstown; the records exist which show that the story of the village's foundation is not as simple as has been suggested. Garden of Troup established a herring station, reputed to be the first on the Moray Firth, but he did not establish the village; he changed the name of an existing village.

The picture is taken en route to St John's Kirk on the modern path, with the full sweep of Gamrie Bay visible. The beach, the Braid Sands, is a significant feature. As a routeway from the village to the Kirk, situated out of shot on the left, its attractions are clear. It is also worth noting that, west of Gamrie Bay, this is the last sizeable sandy beach before Banff. The Craigandargity reef is seen here at high tide.

The beach at Gardenstown is not named on any map but it has a name: the Braid Sands. Some locals believe this means 'Broad Sands'. It is possible, however, that the 'broad' is being used in the Scandinavian sense of 'route way', as in Broad Street. There are several Broad Streets in northeastern Scotland in: Dingwall, Fraserburgh, Peterhead and Aberdeen. The beach at Gamrie was on the route from the village of Powieston, later Gardenstown, to the parish church which sits above the west end of the beach. The estate plan of 1767 clearly shows a path to the church winding up the steep slope at the end of the beach. Although still extant within living memory (John O'Neill, pers. comm.) the path has disappeared.

The real 'Lion's Head'? Picture taken from the sea to the east of Crovie.

We must also be aware that cartographers have made mistakes. One map shows the Snook at the point of Gamrie Head, whereas, in reality it is half way between Gardenstown and Crovie. I am not convinced that the positioning of St John's Stone on the First Edition map is accurate; the map shows the stone not below the church or beside St John's Well but nearer the point, beyond the Muckle Wife. I have already mentioned that I can see absolutely no likeness of a lion at Lion's Head, whether viewed from land or sea but, just off Crovie Head, I have seen the 'Lion Rock', an unmistakable lion's head-shaped rock that is not named on any map.

APPENDIX 4

PRINCIPAL MAPS and PLANS CONSULTED

Maps and plans, ancient and modern, are endlessly fascinating. They are essential resources for understanding places, where the name may have changed or indeed the 'place' disappeared. The information about patterns of settlement and topography has been fundamental to the research for this book.

For those undertaking historical research, arguably the most useful starting points are Ordnance Survey (OS) maps (all editions), the National Library of Scotland (NLS) website (maps.nls.uk), and the Atlas of Scottish History to 1707 edited by McNeill and MacQueen (in Bibliography; see for example Baronies, lordships & earldoms (page 203) or Administrative regions (page 27)).

The fortunate researcher will find that these sources are complemented by historic local maps and plans, prepared by a range of surveyors, with the latter in local or national archives. The lists below are not in order of priority.

List of Maps

OS 1:50000 1st Series; 29 Banff, 30 Fraserburgh and Peterhead

OS 1:25000 Explorer; 426 Banff Macduff & Turriff

OS 6" County Series 1869; Banffshire Sheets V, VI, XI, XII

OS 25" First Edition 1871; Banff Sheet VI.6 (Gamrie)

Bartholomew Half Inch Series 1972; 56 Buchan and Strathbogie

Bartholomew 1912 Survey Atlas of Scotland Plate 48

Pont, Timothy: Manuscript Map 10 Buchan (NLS, ca.1590)

Janssen, Jan: Scotia Provinciae intra Fluvium Taum et Murra Fryth (Amsterdam 1659)

Gordon of Straloch, Robert: Scotia Antiqua (Blaeu, Amsterdam 1654)

Morden, Robert: Scotland (London 1695)

Morden, Robert: A Mapp of Scotland made by R Gorgon, corrected and improved by R Morden (London 1687)

Visscher, Nicolaes: Exactissima Regni Scotiae Tabula (Amsterdam 1689)

Mercator, Gerhard: Scotica Regnum (Duisberg 1595)

Coronelli, Vincenzo: Scotia (Venice 1696)

Hondins, Heidrik: Scotia (Amsterdam 1662, original 1636)

Kaerius, Petrus [van der Keare, Pieter]: The Eastern Part of Scotland (ca.1605) in John Speed's Atlas (London 1676)

Taylor, George and Skinner, Andrew: A General Map of the Roads, made out of Actual Surveys (London 1766)

New Statistical Account: Map of Banffshire, Map of Aberdeenshire (Edinburgh 1845)

Pratt, J B: Map of the District of Buchan (in Pratt's Buchan 1858)

Robertson, T: Aberdeen, Banff, Kincardine 1822

Thomson, John: Aberdeen & Banff in Atlas of Scotland 1826

Plans in Archives

DD 21/1/47 (19th Century) Plans of Farms on Troup Estate (Aberdeenshire Archives)

MS 2626 Home, John: Estate Map of Troup 1767 (Aberdeen University Archives)

MS 3175/RHP 31097 Plan of lands adjoining march between estate of Melrose and Troup 1856 (Aberdeen University Archives)

Ten Merk Lands of Northfield 1811(?) (McDonald Collection, Aberdeen University)

Plan of Baronies of Down & Alva (McDonald Collection, Aberdeen University)

Ray, John: Plan of Troup (date uncertain, see Fort Fiddes Reconsidered chapter)

Admiralty Chart (East from Banff) 1834 (Glasgow University Archives)

TIMELINE

The timeline below is a much-edited version of the one developed and used during the research. Uncertainty about the actual date is indicated with '?'.

Hopefully it still provides a useful link between what was happening in Troup and the chronology of wider events in Scotland. Certainly the full version was an indispensible tool.

YEAR	TROUP	BUCHAN / MORAY	SCOTLAND
1130		David I imposes his authority on the North	David I defeats rebels at Stracathro (Angus, Earl of Moray, and Malcolm)
1136			Melrose Abbey founded with monks from Rievaulx Abbey
1150	Grant of Lethnot by Robert Corbet to Kinloss Abbey?	Foundation of Kinloss Abbey; David I in Moray/Aberdeen	
1153			Death of David I at Carlisle. Malcolm IV (age 12) King of Scots
1165			Death of Malcolm IV. William (the Lion) King of Scots
1170			Charters by Robert and Walter Corbet granting land to Melrose Abbey
1178		Grant of Inverugie to Arbroath Abbey by Ralf le Neym	William I founds Abbey of Arbroath
1189	Grant of church of Gamrie by William I to Arbroath Abbey?		
1205			William Comyn justiciar of Scotland. Famine and severe winter in early months.
1210		William Comyn becomes earl of Buchan	Rainstorms, bad harvests, rivers in spate
1214			Death of William I. Alexander II King of Scots
1215		Uprising/rebellion in Ross and Moray	
1219		William Comyn founds Deer Abbey	
1226	Confirmation of grant of lands of Lethnot by Alexander II		
1233		Death of William Comyn, succeeded by son Alexander	Succession of very cold winters and great frosts
1249			Alexander II dies on Kerrera. Alexander III (age 8) King
1251			Comyn family attain key roles in government
1252			Major drought across British Isles
1258			Volcanic eruption followed by cooling
1263			King orders repairs and strengthening of castles on East and West coast
1264		Richard de Strathern first recorded Sheriff of Banff	

YEAR	TROUP	BUCHAN / MORAY	SCOTLAND
1273		Kingedward Castle mentioned as chief seat of Comyns	
1286			Death of Alexander III at Kinghorn
1289		John Comyn succeeds Alexander (his father) as earl of Buchan	
1290		Royal castle at Banff, Robert Gray castellan of Banff	Death of Maid of Norway in Orkney
1292			John Balliol King of Scots
1293			Severe dearth of food, and famine
1296	Possibly Hamelin de Trop signatory of Ragman Roll		War between John Balliol and Edward. Defeat and submission of John.
1297		Murray rebellion; Wallace supporters active in north-east, Duffus Castle destroyed (Reginald le Chen)	Battle of Stirling Bridge
1298			William Wallace Guardian. Battle of Falkirk
1303		Edward I in north-east, Banff (Sept 4th), Cullen (Sept 5th)	
1304	Hamelin of Troup did homage to Edward I at St Andrews	Duncan de Frendraught is Keeper of King's (Edward I) Forest of Enzie	
1305	Petitions of Hamelin of Troup to Edward I	Walter de Berkley appointed sheriff of Banff (by Edward)	Wallace executed (August); Reginald le Chen justiciar north of the Grampians
1306	Hamelin of Troup reported to be with Bruce. Hamelin in list of Scottish landowners forfeited by Edward I	Grant to Sir Duncan de Frendraught's valet of 13s 4d. (19th June) from Edward I, plus grant to Duncan	John Comyn killed at Dumfries (February); Robert Bruce made king of Scots at Scone (March).
1308		Battle of Inverurie (May) Dundarg Castle destroyed by Bruce followers. Herschip of Buchan; Death of John Comyn earl of Buchan	Poor harvest
1309		Sir Robert Keith granted Aden	Robert Bruce's parliament, Poor harvest followed by famine
1314		Grant by Edward II to Margery widow of Duncan de Ferndraught (£43)	Battle of Bannockburn. Poor Harvest.
1319	Reference to charter for Lethnot in court case of 1537		
1320	Hamelin of Troup accused, but acquitted, of being part of the Soules conspiracy.		Declaration of Arbroath; hereditary role of marischal confirmed to Keiths at Perth Parliament
1323			13 year truce between Scotland and England begins
1328	Hamelin de Trupp is Sheriff of Banff		Edward III resumes his claim to Scotland
1329			Death of Robert I; accession of infant David II
1331			Full coronation and anointment of David II at Scone. William Buttergask is Clerk to Kitchen. Famine
1332	Papal letter giving prebend to Hamelin de Troup		Battle of Dupplin Moor, defeat of Bruce forces by Edward Balliol and Henry Beaumont (Aug); Balliol crowned at Scone (Sept); Disinherited force beaten at Annan, Balliol flees (Dec).

YEAR	TROUP	BUCHAN / MORAY	SCOTLAND
1333		Dundarg Castle rebuilt	Edward III wins Halidon Hill battle (July)
1334		Successful siege of Dundarg Castle	David II seeks refuge in France; Andrew Buttergask depute justiciar north of the Forth
1335	Death of Hamelin (before Feb.)?	David II's party overrun north east	Murray(Guardian) defeats David Strathbogie at Battle of Culblean
1336		Earldom of Moray wasted by Edward III; Aberdeen burned; north-east ravaged	
1337	Grant of pension by English king to Elyne, widow of Hamelin de Troup	Andrew Buttergask is Depute Chamberlain, holds justice ayre in Elgin	
1340			Famine
1341			David II returns to Scotland, landing at Inverbervie
1342	Andrew Buttergask granted barony of Troup by David II	Sir Philip Meldrum sheriff of Banff	
1345	Papal letter granting petition for Hamelin de Trup for church of Inchbrioc		
1346	Andrew Buttergask killed at battle of Neville's Cross	Various Keiths killed at Neville's Cross	Disastrous defeat of Scots army; David II captured and held till 1357
1349			Outbreak of plague in Scotland, loss of one-third of population
1357	Charter by William Troup, son and heir of John of Troup, giving lands of Cragy in Kincardine		Ransom and return of David II (October 6)
1361			Second outbreak of plague
1362		Aberdour as part of Douglas holdings	
1365		John of Bothwell granted thanage of Doune	
1369		Charter to Hugo Ross and Margaret Barclay re Doune	
1371			Death of David II; accession of Robert Stewart as Robert II
1375	Latest date of marriage of Robert Keith to heiress of Troup?	Charters to Robert Keith for lands in Kincardine	
1379			Third outbreak of plague
1380		Keiths inherit Inverugie (from Cheynes) by marriage	
1382		Alexander Stewart (Wolf of Badenoch) becomes earl of Buchan through marriage	
1385		Grant of land of Melros to Janet of Barclay by her brother Andrew	
1390			Death of Robert II; accession of Robert III
1391		Charter from William Keith, marischal, to his son Alexander of Glencuthil	
1392			Keiths acquire Dunottar

YEAR	TROUP	BUCHAN / MORAY	SCOTLAND
1394			Birth of James I
1395		James Lindsay/Robert Keith feud; relief of Fyvie Castle	
1396	Sir Robert de Keith present at Justice Ayre at Aberdeen 5 Feb 96/97	Robert III grants lands of Glendowachy to his uncle James, earl of Buchan	
1402		Isabel, countess of Mar, gives Alexander Keith of Grandoun the lordship of Glendowachy	
1406	Charter to Robert Keith of Troup of lands and barony of Troup	John Stewart, second son of Robert duke of Albany (Regent), made earl of Buchan(September)	James I becomes king succeeding Robert III. James a prisoner of the English
1408	Robert Keith of Troup succeeds father as marischal; resigns Troup		1407/8-one of the 'great winters'.
1411		Battle of Harlaw; settlement of feud between Keiths and Irvines of Drum	
1413	Charter giving John Keith the lands and barony of Troup	Alexander Keith gives Patrick Ogilvie and Christian, his wife, his lands and barony of Doun	
1422		Charter to Patrick Ogilvie and Christian his wife of lands of Glencuthil	Very cold winter
1423		John earl of Buchan departs for France; grants lordship of Kingedward to William Forbes	
1426		King confirms gifts from Archibald earl of Douglas to his brother James of Balveny of baronies of Aberdour and Rattray.	
1428		Confirmation charter for Glencuthil from James I	
1430		Title of Lord Keith created by James I	
1434			Very cold winter
1437			Murder of James I; accession of James II. Very cold winter followed by famine in 1438
1447	John Keith of Troup is a witness to a transcript		
1450		Dundarg as castle of Black Douglases; confirmation by James II of Aberdour to William Douglas	1450s-famine years and crop failures
1454	Charter by John Keith of Troup of lands in Kincardineshire		Huntly changed family name fdrom Seton to Gordon
1458		Title Earl Marischal created by James II	
1460			Death of James II at siege of Roxburgh. Accession of James III.
1462	John Keith of Troup resigns the estate and barony of Troup; gets new charter for the ten merk lands and barony of Northfield.		

YEAR	TROUP	BUCHAN / MORAY	SCOTLAND
1467	Death of John Keith of Troup?	Charter from King of lands of Doun to James Stewart & Margaret Ogilvy; Northfield to James Keith	
1473			Birth of James IV
1478		Charter from James III to his uncle James earl of Buchan of the lands of Glendowachy	
1483		Northfield to John Keith, brother of James	Conspiracy by Albany against King
1484		Charter confirming church of Gamrie and Arbroath Abbey	
1488			Death of James III at Sauchieburn; accession of James IV
1491		Walter Barclay de Tolly succeeds his father John Barclay as flar of Cullen (castle)	Very poor harvest due to summer and autumn rains
1494	Charter to William Keith of barony of Troup, confirmed by James IV		
1500	Rental of Lethnot is 6 merks	Alexander earl of Buchan succeeds father in Glendowachy	Aberdeen forbids trade with north parties until north east Scotland is free from plague
1501		Northfield to Archibald Keith; Alexander earl of Buchan is sheriff of Banff	Rising price of grain due to crop failures
1503		James IV confirms charter from Alexander earl of Buchan to William, lord Ruthven, of lands and barony of Glencuthil	
1504		Glencuthil and Auchmeden to Margaret Ogilvy, widow of James earl of Buchan	
1509		Castlehil at Kingedward to Lord Forbes	
1511	William Keith of Troup is witness to a charter		
1513	William Keith of Troup killed at Flodden; Gilbert Keith obtains barony of Troup		James IV killed at Flodden; accession of James V
1518	Patrick Cheyne of Esslemont vassal of Abbot of Kinloss for Lethnot with rent of 10 merks		
1521	Gilbert Keith of Troup is a witness		
1525	Lease to Gilbert Keith and Elizabeth Forbes his wife	Charter of lands of Earl Marischal includes Troup	Food shortages after autumn rains
1527	Instrument of assignation by Gilbert Keith of Troup to Isabel Forbes his wife	Northfield to John Keith	
1528		James V confirms to John earl of Buchan the barony of Glendowachy or Down	Escape of young James V from Douglases; end of minority.
1529	Gilbert Keith of Troup is a witness in a court case at Aberdeen		

YEAR	TROUP	BUCHAN / MORAY	SCOTLAND
1532	Tack to Gilbert Keith of Troup, Isobel Forbes his spouse and William their son		
1534		James earl of Buchan gives Andrew Baird lands of Glencuthil and Auchmedden	
1535		Marriage of 4th earl Huntly and Elizabeth Keith	
1537	Hearing re Lethnot lands involving Gilbert Keith of Troup and Patrick Cheyne of Esslemont		
1538		Charter from James V uniting barony of Aberdour with barony of Borthwick	
1542			Battle of Solway Moss; death of James V; accession of Mary
1550	Marriage of Elizabeth Keith daughter of Gilbert Keith of Troup to George, second son of Andrew Baird of Auchmedden	Northfield to William Keith. Dundarg Castle refortified, Aberdour to Alexander Fraser of Philorth	
1552	Gilbert Keith of Troup is a witness		
1553	Possible date of Mason's Mark in kitchen at Troup		
1560			Parliament legislates protestant reformation of Church of Scotland
1562		Charter to James earl of Mar and his wife Agnes Keith for lands of Glencuthil and Auchmedden	
1568			Flight of Mary to England
1571		Patrick Cheyne of Esslemont takes possession of barony of Aberdour	
1574		Barclay arms in stone at castle of Cullen; date of Barclays move to Towie?	
1577	Agreement of Alexander Keith and Patrick Cheyne	John Keith brother of George, Earl Marischal contracted to Elizabeth oldest daughter of Alexander Keith of Troup	
1578		Northfield to John Keith	James VI takes over from regent
1580	Alexander Keith of Troup a burgess of Aberdeen		
1587	John Keith is fiar of Troup; reference to Isobel Keith daughter of John Keith of Troup; caution re behaviour of William Gordon of Gight to John Keith of Troup	Charter by James VI (#1341) to George Earl Marischal confirming Troup (inter alia)	Execution of Mary (Feb). Tryst between earl of Huntly and Earl Marischal leads to slaughter of Keith.
1589	2 cautions re behaviour of John Keith of Troup		

154

YEAR	TROUP	BUCHAN / MORAY	SCOTLAND
1592	Reference to John Keith of Troup, third in line	Inverugie charter (304) gives lands of Keiths, including Troup.	
1594	Complaint before Privy Council against John Keith of Troup and others		Battle of Glenlivet (Oct).
1596	Robert son of Alexander Keith of Troup is a burgess of Aberdeen		
1598	John Keith, brother of George earl Marischal has a charter for Crovie; dies unmarried		
1600	Date of wadset on lands of Troup from George Earl Marischal to Gilbert Keith of Troup		
1601			Very cold summer following volcanic ash cloud
1602	Complaint before Privy Council against John Keith of Troup and others		
1603		Northfield to William Keith	Union of the Crowns
1610	Gilbert Keith of Troup - discharge of wadset		
1612		Francis son of John Keith of Northfield cautioner	
1630		Grant by Charles 1 of the ten merk lands and barony of Northfield to Sir William Keith of Ludquharn; Alexander Fraser younger of Philorth granted Aberdour etc. to Lord Pitsligo	Death of John Gordon at Frendraught
1632	Lands of Troup granted to Sir James Gordon of Lesmoir		
1640		Northfield to George Keith	Robert Gordon of Straloch describing Moray
1645			Last outbreak of plague
1651			Scotland incorporated into the English Commonwealth and Protectorate
1654	Gardens acquire Troup		
1712		Northfield to Alexander Keith	
1754		Northfield to George Keith	
1777	Visit by Williams to Cullykhan		
1789		Northfield to George Keith	
1793	Francis Garden succeeds to Troup		Reference to Lt James Fiddes at Barbados
1803	Construction of Fort Fiddes		
1897	Current Troup House built		

BIBLIOGRAPHY

This booklist contains those texts specifically referenced in the text, together with others that provided essential background reading.

Bain, J (ed) 1881-7 *Calendar of Documents relating to Scotland Vol. 1,2,3,5* Edinburgh.

Bannerman, W 1895 'On the Extinction of Gaelic in Buchan and lower Banffshire' Banffshire Journal Banff.

Bannerman, W 1897 *The Thanage of Glendowachy* Banffshire Journal.

Bannatyne Club, 1837 *Registrum Episcopatum Moraviensis* Edinburgh.

Barclay, H F 1933 *A History of the Barclay Family 1067-1933 Part II* London.

Barrow, G W S 1976 *Robert Bruce and the Community of the Realm of Scotland* Edinburgh.

Barrow, G W S 1980 *The Anglo Norman Era in Scottish History* Oxford.

Barrow, G W S 1984 'Land Routes: The Medieval Evidence' in Fenton A & Stell G (eds) *Loads and Roads in Scotland and Beyond: Road Transport over 6000 years* 49-66 Edinburgh.

Barrow, G W S 1999 *The Charters of David I* Woodbridge.

Barrow, G W S 2003 *Kingship & Unity: Scotland 1000-1306* London.

Beam, A 2009 'The Umfravilles: Political Leadership on the Rise, 1100-1307' in *History Scotland March/April 2009.*

Black, G F 1946 *The Surnames of Scotland* New York.

Bliss, W H 1893 *Calendar of Entries in the Papal Registers Relating to Great Britain & Ireland Vol 1 1342 – 1419* London.

Boardman, S 1996 *The Early Stewart Kings Robert II and Robert III 1371 – 1400* East Linton.

Brown, C 2002 *The Second Scottish Wars of Independence 1332-63* Stroud.

Brown, K M 1986 *Bloodfeud in Scotland 1573-1625* Edinburgh.

Brown, M 1994 *James I* East Linton.

Brown, M 1996 'Regional Lordship in North East Scotland: The Badenoch Stewarts II' in *Northern Scotland* Vol 16 31-54 Old Aberdeen.

Brown, M 1998 *The Black Douglases* East Linton.

Brown, M 2004 *The Wars of Scotland 1214 – 1371, The New Edinburgh History of Scotland Volume 4* Edinburgh.

Bulloch, J M (ed) 1903/7 *House of Gordon* New Spalding Club Aberdeen.

Bulloch, J M 1934 The Bairds of Auchmeden' in Transactions of the Buchan Field Club 177-203 Peterhead.

Burton, J H and others (ed) 1877 *Register of the Privy Council of Scotland* Vol V, VI Edinburgh.

Cordiner, Rev C 1780 *Antiquities and Scenery of the North of Scotland* London.

Cramond, W 1903 *The Records of Elgin 1234-1800 Vol 1* Aberdeen.

Coutts, J 1922 *The Anglo Norman Peaceful Invasion of Scotland* Edinburgh.

Coventry, M 2001 *The Castles of Scotland (3rd edition)* Musselburgh

Cowan, I B 1967 *Parishes of Medieval Scotland* Edinburgh.

Dawson, A 2009 *So Foul and Fair a Day: A History of Scotland's Weather and Climate* Edinburgh

Dawson, J E A 2007 *Scotland Re-Formed 1488-1587 The New Edinburgh History of Scotland Volume 6* Edinburgh.

Dennison, P, Ditchburn, D & Lynch, M (eds) *Aberdeen Before 1800: A New History* East Linton.

Douglas, F 1782 *A General Description of the East Coast of Scotland from Edinburgh to Cullen* Paisley.

Douglas, Sir R 1813 *The Peerage of Scotland Vol 2* Edinburgh.

Duncan, A A M 1989 *Scotland: The Making of the Kingdom* Edinburgh.

Duncan, W 1908 'Notes from Banff and Buchan' (1722) in *Macfarlane's Geographical Collections* Vol III, Scottish History Society Vol 43 Edinburgh.

Ferguson, J 1910 *Old Castles of Buchan* Peterhead.

Ferguson, J 1913 *Old Baronies of Buchan* Vol X Transactions Buchan Field Club Peterhead.

Ferrerrii, J 1839 *Historia Abbatum de Kynlos* Bannatyne Club Edinburgh.

Fojut, N and Love, P 1983 'The defences of Dundarg Castle, Aberdeenshire' in *Proc. Soc. Ant. Scot. Vol 113* pp 449-456 Edinburgh.

Forbes, A L 2012 *Trials and Triumphs: The Gordons of Huntly in Sixteenth Century Scotland* Edinburgh.

Geddes, J (ed), 2016 *Medieval Art, Architecture and Archaeology in the Dioceses of Aberdeen and Moray* London

Gordon of Straloch, R 1908 'Annotate and Descriptionem duarum praefecturarum Aberdoniae et Banffiae in Scotia Ultramontana' (1662) in *Macfarlane's Geographical Collections Vol 3* Scottish History Society Vol 43 Edinburgh.

Grant, A 1993 'Thanes and Thanages from the Eleventh to the Fourteenth Century' in Grant,A & Stringer, K J (eds) *Medieval Scotland Crown, Lordship and Community* 39-81 Edinburgh.

Grant, J 1912 *Seafield Correspondence 1685-1708* Scottish History Society Edinburgh.

Grant, J 1922 *Records of the County of Banff 1660-1760* New Spalding Club Aberdeen.

Greig, J C 1970 Excavations at Castle Point, Troup, Banffshire in *Aberdeen University Review Vol XLIII* 274-283 Aberdeen.

Greig, J C 1971 Excavations at Cullykhan, Castle Point, Troup, Banffshire in *Scottish Archaeology Forum Vol 3* 15-21 Edinburgh.

Greig, J C 1972 Cullykhan in *Current Archaeology 72* 227-230 London.

Greig, M 2013 Excavations of an unnamed castle at Cullykhan, Castle Point, Troup in *Proc. Soc. Ant. Scot. Vol 142* 301-328 Edinburgh.

Greig, M K & Greig, J C 1989 'Remains of a 12th Century Structure and other Medieval Remains on the Knoll of Castle Point, Troup (Cullykhan), Banff and Buchan' in *Proc Soc Ant Scot Vol 119* 279-296 Edinburgh.

Groome, F J 1882 *Ordnance Gazetteer of Scotland* (6 volumes) Edinburgh.

Hough, C 2014 'The Green Belt and Beyond: Metaphor in the Landscape' in *Scottish Place Names News No. 37 (Autumn 2014)*

Innes, T 1927 'The First earl Marischal' in *Scottish Historical Review Vol 24* Glasgow.

Innes, T 1936 *The Hays of Delgaty,* Banffshire Field Club Banff.

Kay, J 1837/8 *A Series of Original Portraits and Caricature Etchings by the late John Kay, with Biographical Sketches and Illustrative Anecdotes* Edinburgh.

Kerr-Petersen, M 2016 'Post-Reformation Church Architecture in the Marischal Earldom 1560-1625' in Geddes J (ed) *Medieval Art, Architecture and Archaeology in the Dioceses of Aberdeen and Moray* London

Leith, J Forbes 1909 *The Irvines of Drum* Aberdeen.

Littlejohn, D (ed) 1906 *Records of the Sheriff Court of Aberdeenshire 1598-1649* New Spalding Club Aberdeen.

Lockhart Gordon, P 1830 *Personal Memoirs or Reminiscences At Home and Abroad* London.

Lynch, M (ed) 2001 *The Oxford Companion to Scottish History* Oxford.

McNeill, P G B & MacQueen, H L (eds) 1996 *Atlas of Scottish History to 1707* Edinburgh.

MacDougall, N 1997 *James IV* East Linton.

Macphail, S R 1881, *History of the Religious House of Pluscarden* Edinburgh.

Macquarrie, A 2004 *Medieval Scotland: Kingship and Nation* Stroud.

Masson, D (ed.) 1881, 1882, 1884, *Register of the Privy Council of Scotland Vol IV (1585-92) Vol V (1592-99) Vol VI (1599-1604)*, General Register House Edinburgh.

Milne, J 1886 *King Edward Castle* Banffshire Field Club.

New Spalding Club 1890 *Miscellany of the New Spalding Club* Aberdeen.

New Spalding Club 1891 *Annals of Banff* Aberdeen.

New Spalding Club 1906 *Records of the Sheriff Court of Aberdeenshire Vol II 1598-1649* Aberdeen.

New Statistical Account of Scotland 1845 Vol 13 Edinburgh.

Nicolaisen, W F H 2001 *Scottish Place-Names* Edinburgh

Old Statistical Account 1790-91 Volume XVI Edinburgh

Oram, R 2004 *David I: The King Who Made Scotland* Stroud.

Oram, R 2011 *Dominion and Lordship: Scotland 1070-1230, The New Edinburgh History of Scotland Volume 2* Edinburgh.

Oram, R 2016 'The Medieval Church in the Dioceses of Aberdeen and Moray" in Geddes J (ed) *Medieval Art, Architecture and Archaeology in the Dioceses of Aberdeen and Moray* London.

Ordnance Survey 1868 *Name Book for Banffshire. Chap 14* Edinburgh.

Owen, D D R 1997 *William the Lion: Kingship and Culture 1143-1214* East Linton.

Palgrave, J D 1837 *Documents and Records Illustrating the History of Scotland Vol 1* London.

Paul, Sir J Balfour 1909 *The Scots Peerage* Vol VI Edinburgh.

Paul, Sir J Balfour 1984 *The Register of the Great Seal of Scotland AD 1424-1513* The Scottish Record Society Edinburgh.

Penman, M 1999 A Fell Coniuracion again Robert the douchty King : the Soules conspiracy of 1318- 20 in *Innes Review Vol 50* 25-57 Edinburgh.

Penman, M 2004 *David II 1329 – 71* Edinburgh.

Potter, H 2002 *Bloodfeud: The Stewarts & Gordons at War,* Stroud.

Pratt, J B 1858 *Buchan* Aberdeen (reprinted 1978, Turriff).

Rhind, W 1839 *Sketches of Moray* Edinburgh.

Ritchie, R L G 1954 *The Normans in Scotland* Edinburgh.

Robertson, B 2011 *Lordship and Power in the North of Scotland: The Noble House of Huntly 1603-1690* Edinburgh.

Rogers, C J 2000 *War Cruel and Sharp: English Strategy Under Edward III, 1327 – 1360* Woodbridge.

Royal Scottish Geographical Society 1973 *The Early Maps of Scotland Vol 1* Edinburgh.

Sanderson, M H B 2002 *A Kindly Place: Living in Sixteenth Century Scotland* East Lothian.

Shaw, L 1882 *The History of the Province of Moray Vol 1* Glasgow.

Simpson, G G and Galbraith, J D (eds) 1986 *Calendar of Documents Relating to Scotland Vol V AD 1108 – 1516* Scottish Record Office Edinburgh.

Simpson, W D 1922 'The Architectural History of Huntly Castle' in *Proc. Soc. Ant. Scot. Vol 56* 134-163 Edinburgh.

Simpson, W D 1960 'Dundarg Castle Reconsidered' in *Transactions of the Buchan Club 17* 9-25 Peterhead.

Smith, J W 1964 'The Gardens of Troup' in *Transactions of the Buchan Field Club* Vol XVIII part 1 Peterhead.

Spalding Club 1843 *Collections for a History of the Shires of Aberdeen and Banff* Aberdeen.

Spalding Club, 1845 *Registrum Episcopatus Aberdoniensis Vol 1* Edinburgh.

Spalding Club 1847, 1857, *1862 Illustrations of the Topography and Antiquities of the Shires of Aberdeen and Banff Vol 2,3,4* Aberdeen.

Spalding Club, 1852 *Miscellany of the Spalding Club* Vol V Aberdeen.

Spence, J 1873 *Ruined Castles: Monuments of Former Men in the Vicinity of Banff* Edinburgh.

Stuart, J and Burnett, G (eds) 1878 *The Exchequer Rolls of Scotland* Vol 1 General Register House Edinburgh.

Tayler, A 1937 'The Gardens of Troup' in *Proceedings of the Banffshire Field Club (March 1937)* 2-26 Banff.

Tayler, A and H 1933 *The Valuation for the County of Aberdeen for the year 1667* Third Spalding Club Aberdeen.

Tayler, A and H 1937 *The House of Forbes* Third Spalding Club Aberdeen.

Taylor, A 2016 *The Shape of the State in Medieval Scotland 1124-1290* Oxford.

Taylor, J 1858 *Edward I of England in the North of Scotland* Elgin.

Taylor, J 1891 *The Great Historic Families of Scotland Vol 1* 98-126 London.

Taylor, S with Markus, G 2012 *The Place-Names of Fife Volume 5* Donington.

The Scots Magazine 1804 *Miscellany for 1804* Vol LXVI Edinburgh.

Thomson, J M (ed) 1984 *The Register of The Great Seal of Scotland Vol 1,2,5* Scottish Records Society Edinburgh.

Thornton-Kemsley, G 1972 *Bonnet Lairds* Montrose.

Watson, A 2002 *Place Names, Lands and Lordship in the medieval earldom of Strathearn* (unpublished PhD thesis)

Watson, W J 1926 *The History of the Celtic Place Names of Scotland* Edinburgh.

Watt, D E R (ed) 1996 *Scotichronicon* Vol 7 Aberdeen.

Williams, J 1777 *An Account of Some Remarkable Ancient Ruins, lately discovered in the highlands and northern parts of Scotland* Edinburgh.

Wilson, J M (ed) 1868 *The Imperial Gazetteer of Scotland Vol II* London & Edinburgh.

Yeoman, P A 1988 'Mottes in North East Scotland' in *Scottish Archaeological Review 5* Glasgow

Young, A 1993 'The Earls and Earldom of Buchan in the Thirteenth Century' in Grant, A & Stringer, K J (eds) *Medieval Scotland : Crown, Lordship and Community*, 174-202 Edinburgh.

Young, A 1997 *Robert the Bruce's Rivals: The Comyns 1212 -1314* East Lothian.

Listed below are sources that have been used in this book, together with their locations. Maps and plans are listed in Appendix 4.

National Archives of Scotland

GD 36/308

GD 26/8/989

GD 49/30

GD 57/1/133A

RH6 2445

Acc 6206 IV 5

Aberdeenshire Archives

DD 21 Garden of Troup papers

National Archives (Kew)

CO 267/11 1/222, 1/223

Archives of the University of Aberdeen

MS 3175/1456/2 (Montcoffer Papers)

MS 1027 Uncompleted manuscript relating to the Keith family by Lt Col A Y Cheyne (died July 1935)

National Library of Scotland

maps/nls.uk/military/view/?id=355 - details of survey undertaken at Banff

Masons' Mark Project

www.masonsmarkproject.org.uk

Historic Land Measures: Further Reading

Barrow, G W S 2003 Kingship and Unity: Scotland 1000 – 1306 Appendix A 173-5 Edinburgh

Cramond, W 1901 'Old Scottish Land Measures' in Proceedings of the Banffshire Field Club Banff

Ross, A 2011 The Kings of Alba 14 – 33 Edinburgh

INDEX

The Author

Alex McKay is a native of Banffshire. Born in Buckie, he was brought up in Sandend where he attended the village school before moving on to Fordyce Academy. When Fordyce Academy closed, he transferred to Banff Academy for the remainder of his secondary education. His time there was enjoyable and successful: he was Head Boy and Dux. He went on to take an honours degree in mathematics at Aberdeen University and trained as a teacher at Aberdeen College of Education.

His first teaching appointment was in Perth and he was subsequently promoted to posts in Ellon and Elgin. After secondment to a national project, he moved to Fife where he spent the remainder of his career, initially in the Advisory Service and latterly in the senior management of the Education Service. His final post was Head of Education. He is now retired and lives in Scone.

He is married to Jennifer who shares his enthusiasm for archaeology. They have one son, Neil.

While at Banff Academy he took part in excavations at Cullykhan and Lundin Links and, so, began a lifelong interest in archaeology and history. In retirement, he has returned to practical archaeology and has excavated as a volunteer on a number of digs, mainly in the east and north of Scotland with Glasgow University, the National Museum of Scotland, and Aberdeen University. He is a Fellow of the Society of Antiquaries of Scotland, and a member of numerous local and national historical and cultural societies.

When not actively involved in excavations or historical research, he enjoys travel and visiting family in Asia and Australia.